Brave

WRITERS AND ARTISTS
WRESTLE WITH GOD, LOVE, DEATH,
AND THE THINGS THAT MATTER

Souls

DOUGLAS TODD

Stoddart

Copyright © 1996 by Douglas Todd

Published in 1996 by Stoddart Publishing Co. Limited

Distributed in Canada by
General Distribution Services Inc.
30 Lesmill Road
Toronto, Canada M3B 2T6
Tel. (416) 445-3333
Fax (416) 445-5967
e-mail Customer.Service@ccmailgw.genpub.com

Distributed in the United States by
General Distribution Services Inc.
85 River Rock Drive, Suite 202
Buffalo, New York 14207
Toll free 1-800-805-1083
Fax (416) 445-5967
e-mail Customer.Service@ccmailgw.genpub.com

Cataloguing in Publication Data available from
the National Library of Canada

ISBN 0-7737-5832-1

These interviews appeared in an earlier form in the *Vancouver Sun*
and are republished here with permission of the *Sun*.

Cover Design: Bill Douglas at the Bang
Text Design: Tannice Goddard

Printed and bound in Canada

Courage is a kind of salvation.
— PLATO

Contents

Acknowledgments

For their support, direct and indirect, in the creation of this book, I thank: the twenty-eight writers and artists who bared their souls; the Canada Council; my tolerant family, Elaine, Nate, Thomas, and Devin; my eclectic family of origin and handy in-laws; Kootenay philosopher Will Morrison; George Hermanson and the far-flung gang; Max Wyman, John Cruickshank, Shelley Fralic, Gary Mason, and Graham Rockingham, editors at the *Vancouver Sun*; my rarely dull *Sun* colleagues, particularly the photographers; editors Lynne Missen and Elizabeth d'Anjou, whose refined taste made this a better book, and Don Bastian, gentlemanly managing editor of Stoddart.

Introduction

Something big is going on in contemporary spirituality. While polls in the United States and Canada consistently show that only about a third of the population regularly attend religious institutions, a staggering 90 percent say they believe in God. North Americans are facing an upheaval in traditional thoughts and customs. And few people are better positioned to help us understand it than our top writers and artists.

This book is the reader's chance to sit down with twenty-eight of North America's most creative souls while they wrestle with God, love, death, and the things that matter. Many of these writers and artists were intimately exposed to Christianity and Judaism in their early years, but only a few still attend religious institutions. None sit in the pews obediently; all are troubled by religious orthodoxy. They follow the truth wherever it may lead.

While the subjects in this book are like many people in the way they are largely searching outside institutional religion, they also stand out from the crowd. Almost all have reputations beyond North America's borders, where they draw widespread admiration from tens of millions of people. *Brave Souls* shows how the hard-won insights of writers and artists such as Carol Shields, Robertson Davies, Alex Colville, Douglas Coupland, and Lynn Johnston influence their creative work. The novels of John Irving and Evelyn Lau deal with the tortured intricacies of moral, sexual, ethnic, and spiritual ambiguity; Loreena McKennitt's spiritual passions captivate audiences all over the world; Robert Munsch's children's books echo his concern for the underdog; Timothy Findley's worldview changed when he experienced the sacred in the vast Arctic; Bruce Cockburn's politics are shaped by the camouflage-design New Testament he keeps in his satchel. Even those who no longer believe in God, like Mordecai Richler and Jane Rule, are searching intently — for a moral code to live by.

The writers and artists in this book believe in a wide range of things: the power of love (romantic, fraternal, erotic, sacrificial, and mystical), the centrality of community, the interrelatedness of all things, the need to get beyond mechanistic science, the lessons of war, devotion to beauty, the reality of evil, openness to the paranormal, the need for ritual, the value of tradition, the necessity to face our dark side, taking a stand, the strength of silence, the possibility (or not) of life beyond death, the need to be curious, the mystical strength of nature, and the reality of that most unfashionable quality, goodness.

These twenty-eight writers and artists show how the real spiritual story today is not what particular religious group we belong to, which doctrine we profess, or which system of philosophy we follow. It is about how we cobble together meaning in our lives. What do we really believe when we suddenly wake up at 3 a.m.?

It would be an understatement to say I was nervous before asking personal spiritual questions of these writers and artists (for the sake of brevity, in the term "artist," I include visual artists, musical performers, comic-strip creators, and film directors). Some have been my heroes since my late teens and early twenties. I remember dancing to Bruce Cockburn's early song "Burn, Baby Burn" in our co-op student house while attending the University of British Columbia. I remember being captivated by the magic of Robertson Davies' *Fifth Business* when I was a member of a Toronto theater group called "Creation 2." I have long been entranced by the cosmic order in Alex Colville's paintings, awestruck at Bill Reid's giant Haida sculpture of a raven cracking open the clamshell that contained the world's first humans, and riveted by the karmic forces John Irving suggests are at work in *The World According to Garp*. For some of the others, my respect and affection (though not always agreement) have come in more recent years, particularly during our time together.

My trepidation was increased by the audacity of my task: to ask them to bare their most intimate convictions about what matters. This, when a lot of them had become used to being interviewed about such banal subjects as whether they wrote with a typewriter or computer, or how they handled their rising stardom. While some prominent writers and artists turned down requests for interviews, others in this book only took part because they were intrigued by its unusual subject matter. I found that although my interviewees had rarely been asked before about their spirituality, most had pondered questions of religion and ethics all their lives. Three of them — Robert Munsch, Ann Copeland, and Barry Lopez — trained for Catholic orders. Many sang in church choirs or had born-again experiences. Nearly all attended church or synagogue in their youth, and some, like Susan Aglukark and Tony Hillerman, have to this day not let attendance completely slip.

Still, many were leery at first about getting into the touchy subject of religion and ethics. In some cases it took months, even years, to set up these face-to-face sessions. After we met, however, all stepped out boldly onto this uncharted profile territory. In the end, they appeared delighted with the chance to speak about what mattered. Some displayed great vulnerability, and I could not help but appreciate their remarkable candor.

The conversations took place across the continent: in Alex Colville's immaculate sunroom in Wolfville, Nova Scotia; at a sidewalk restaurant in Toronto near where Loreena McKennitt once played harp music as a busker; at a conference of Bible scholars Paul Verhoeven attended in Edmonton; at ex-prostitute Evelyn Lau's favorite tony Vancouver restaurant; at Robert Fulghum's warehouse-sized studio on the Seattle waterfront; in Nick Bantock's hobbit-like enclave in the West Coast's evergreen forest; in a Vancouver hotel courtyard before Carol Shields's son was about to be married.

I was raised in an atheist home, where I picked up some of the advantages of atheism: skepticism and a critical mind. When Christian missionaries would come to the grounds of Argyle high school in North Vancouver, my friends would pick me to go out and debate them. I never had bad religion foisted on me, so I didn't rebel against religion the way most teenagers do.

I went in the opposite direction. Late in high school, I began learning, through a teacher, that not all religious people are kooks. I became so much persuaded to the contrary, in fact, that I wound up receiving a bachelor of arts in world religions at the University of British Columbia and later studied in California at the School of Theology at Claremont and Claremont Graduate School. I found questions of spirituality and ethics, and the little-appreciated discipline of the philosophy of religion, to be among the most fascinating subjects on the planet. The secular media and popular culture are slowly coming to similar conclusions. The word "spirituality" is becoming part of the common lexicon — bumping aside, for better or for worse, "religion" with its connotations of institutional attachment.

During my first decade in journalism, I covered everything from politics and murder trials to movies and music. Although the religion beat has until recently been low status at many newspapers, reserved for the office drunk or the new kid who isn't in a position to say no, I decided I wanted to renew my passion for religious issues about five years ago and proposed a religion and ethics beat for the *Vancouver Sun*, the city's only broadsheet newspaper.

Combining my love for spiritual exploration with a fondness for the arts, I soon thought it would be illuminating to find out what noted writers and artists, the guiding lights of our culture, had to say about life's big religious and moral questions. In the midst of what Hindus call the "householder" phase of life, raising three young boys with my wife, Elaine, it's been a privilege to, in effect, go back to school and learn directly from some of the most inspiring people on the continent. Some of the micro-profiles in this book began with pieces that ran in my Saturday column in the *Vancouver Sun*. The Canada Council supported the idea of producing a book and gave me the time and travel money to expand the project.

As I got to know these writers and artists over the past few years, patterns emerged. I realized they could be roughly categorized according to four classic approaches to religion: atheism, agnosticism, identification with a tradition, and eclectic mysticism. The only classic approach I didn't encounter was unquestioning obedience to religious authority. As Alex Colville suggests, this approach is a non-starter for any truly creative person, who feels compelled to shatter outmoded forms, whether in art, literature, or belief.

In the first part, we meet the atheists. Atheism is a tough choice today. Although this is supposedly a secular age, in many quarters, particularly in politics and business, a subtle stigma still attaches itself to atheists. About 10 percent of North Americans tell census takers they have "no religion," but most are vague about what that means.

Fewer than 1 percent actually declare themselves to be atheist.

The five writers and artists in this book who are atheists are proud of their choices. Often justifiably angry about their religious upbringing, they have iconoclastically concluded that standard religious faith crushes human dignity, promotes self-righteousness, threatens authentic living, and stifles the imagination. However, their lack of belief in God hasn't led to a denial of deep meaning in life. The atheists in this book may ask tough questions and puncture illusions; but they're convinced life can be lived with purpose.

There are great differences among these five atheists. W. P. Kinsella, for instance, is a self-confessed cynic, while Jane Rule is a compassionate activist who puts her money where her heart is. Robert Munsch could be called a secular mystic. But the links among these five are also provocative. It is perhaps not surprising that four of the five — Rule, Reid, Richler, and Kinsella — hail from British Columbia or Quebec, which polls show are the most secular provinces in Canada. And it is peculiar that four of the five — all but Munsch — share ill health. Is there some connection between chronic sickness and rejection of belief in God? More significant, perhaps, is the fact that four of these atheists make humor a large part of their life and work. Munsch, Kinsella, and Richler all defy the powers that be with irreverence in their work, while Reid is a sly debunker in private life. In the face of an overwhelming cosmos, humor can bring things down to earth and provide a sense of proportion.

Through their creative imaginations and their relentless curiosity, they are like the trickster figure in North American native mythology. Most of these atheists still maintain wonder about the world. They realize the role of the artist is to help us transcend our own sense of insignificance and live with some adventure and zest. As we will see, some of their beliefs are not as far removed as they may think from the subjects I have grouped in the last part as those who are creating a new spirituality.

The group I have christened "The Doubters" doesn't take a clear-cut stand on the ultimate nature of reality. These six writers and artists honestly struggle with fundamental questions of faith and values. In some ways they are this book's Everyman and Everywoman. Like Thomas Huxley, who in 1869 coined the word "agnostic" to describe those who repudiate both traditional Judeo-Christian theism and doctrinaire atheism, the writers and artists in this section are agnostics because they haven't been convinced either way. Ours may be an age of agnosticism, with the vast majority of North Americans telling pollsters they believe in God, but with far fewer actually feeling positive enough to join a religious institution.

Agnostics come in many varieties. Douglas Coupland yearns for a system of thought that fosters kindness, but doesn't want to be caught in the same room with people who believe they've found the way and the truth. Ethnobotanist Wade Davis, author of *The Serpent and the Rainbow*, yearns for faith after witnessing amazing paranormal phenomena among Voodoo acolytes of Haiti. Director Paul Verhoeven, who is preparing to make a film about the *real* Jesus, sometimes wishes his stubborn skepticism would just go away so he could get over his terrifying fear of death. Since Evelyn Lau's cosmology changes every month, it's hard for her to be convinced about the reality of love, let alone a monotheistic God. Crime writer Laurence Gough began questioning his atheism when his father died. He is experiencing tentative beginnings of religious faith, along with a growing understanding of forgiveness. Finally, some doubters, like John Irving, have elevated their agnosticism into an art form. He was taught in a liberal Christian school and has no desire to shake all vestiges of the tolerant spirituality of his youth.

The agnostics find fundamentalism unacceptable in any sphere, be it religion, politics, economics, or morality. Yet they are not without a sense of awe, which is a kind of faith. John Irving, Wade Davis, and Douglas Coupland are among the many who don't believe doubt necessarily cancels out faith. They are enlivened by possibility.

The third part of the book concerns those whom I call "The New Ancients," who maintain some loyalty to organized faith. The writers and artists in this section hold on to the wisdom of the ancients. They respect tradition — though they do not accept it blindly.

These six writers and artists continue to find support and inspiration in a 2,000-year-old tradition. Some attend church; others do not, but all maintain a Christian identity — and definitely not because it is fashionable or comfortable. After much study and consideration, after rejecting the orthodox forms of faith that overemphasized guilt and sinfulness, Bruce Cockburn, Ann Copeland, Lynn Johnston, Tony Hillerman, and Susan Aglukark still find Christianity gives them the strength to take risks, to go further than they thought they could go. Robertson Davies, whom I interviewed a year before his death, also resided in this category.

The new ancients don't write off the strife-ridden Christian tradition because it has flaws. What tradition older than yesterday doesn't? They show some humility in the way they avoid trying to reinvent the spiritual wheel. They don't grab on to something new simply because it is exotic, although they are ready to learn from anyone. Jesus teaches them to be ready for creative transformation, open to the transcendent in all aspects of life: ritual, music, literature, nature, sexuality, art, and people.

Roughly 35 percent of North Americans tell pollsters they consider themselves Christian, but rarely attend church, and this is the situation of most of this group of writers and artists. These men and women are helping create a new form of Christianity, which, as Cockburn says, is not about rules or even about hard-and-fast definitions of God. It is about becoming co-creators with God. The personalities examined in this section shatter the stereotype of uptight Christians observing ritual niceties. These people see Jesus as a person who challenged the established order and hated the sanctimonious ways of the law-bound Pharisees.

Their Christianity provides them with a strong, clear, ethical vision, based on the simple but revolutionary ideals of loving your brother and sister and loving your neighbor as yourself. Cockburn's politics are often the opposite of those pushed by the religious right. He fights for homosexual rights and against the dominance of multinational corporations, and believes it may be justified, in certain circumstances, to toss a Molotov cocktail through the window of a pornography parlor. If Catholic Hillerman were Pope, he'd hold a giant garage sale at the Vatican and give all the proceeds to the poor.

The most traditional Christian among this group also counters clichés: Aglukark is neither white nor European. The Inuit singer is a political leader in the struggle to establish an Inuit homeland in the new Arctic territory of Nunavut. Her Christianity gives her the stamina to spend hours upon hours with victims of abuse. But she is harshly critical of guilt-mongering Christians, including her own parents.

These new ancients clearly show that the general understanding of what constitutes a Christian is far too narrow. Davies attended the Anglican Church, but was long attracted to an early Christian heresy known as Gnosticism. He was also a student of astrology. Copeland and Johnston consider themselves Christians, although they question whether Jesus was literally the son of God. They are among a growing number who find atonement theology, the belief that salvation would be impossible if Jesus had not died on the cross to atone for all of humanity's sins, a doctrinal stumbling block that unnecessarily turns many away from Christian faith.

A dramatic reevaluation of the person of Jesus is taking place among these writers and artists — as well as among the non-Christians in the last section of the book, who are inspired by the figure of Jesus. Many cite the gospel passage in which Jesus overturns the tables of the moneylenders in the temple as a key example of how being spiritual does not mean being bland. They point to this passage to show that political protest has a long, respected tradition. They also highlight it to counter the worn-out idea that spiritual perfection means being immutable and unaffected by the world. Jesus showed that the divine embraces real, passionate emotions, including anger. These writers and artists support a Christianity that says God is intimately related to the world's sorrows and joys.

The largest group of writers and artists in this book I have called "The Emerging Mystics." It is no coincidence that many of the eleven subjects in this section live amid nature. Nick Bantock and Barry Lopez are buried deep in the West Coast forest; Farley Mowat is perched above the gray Atlantic Ocean; Timothy Findley, Loreena McKennitt, and Robert Bly make their homes on rural acreages; and Alex Colville has a place overlooking the sea. Nature is a key source of their emerging mysticism.

They are not necessarily more spiritually sophisticated than the new ancients, or, for that matter, the atheists and doubters. I have grouped them together because they are all mystics who refuse to identify themselves with a single, central source of spiritual inspiration. They're drawn to nature in part because it has no doctrine. When unspoiled by human technology and arrogance, what better place is there to witness how the universe really unfolds? In nature, especially animals, these writers and artists see intricate order at work. They realize the universe is not a machine. They see the sacred embedded in nature's creative evolutionary process.

Although the power and complexity of nature is the key spiritual inspiration for these writers and artists, they have walked other eclectic paths to wisdom. Their diverse influences include Buddhism, Hinduism, Taoism, post-classical Christianity, Quakerism, mythologist Joseph Campbell, Celtic paganism, astrophysics, biology, Plato, Aristotle, Jewish mysticism, medieval Saint-worship, process philosophy, Gnosticism, Romantic poets, Sufism, Egyptian esthetics, Arthurian legends, and Carl Jung. Along with the new ancients, they're redefining divinity, which they variously describe as God, the sacred, the holy, the motivator, *duende*, Eros, the dynamic, and the transcendent.

They don't agree on life's big questions. Findley allows for some form of life after death, while Carol Shields doesn't — at least not for now. On the surface, at least, some of their ethics seem to clash. Colville calls himself a conservative while Mowat is a democratic socialist; yet both are committed to compassion. Some, such as Sylvia Fraser, push the edges of open-mindedness, coming close to a state of mind cynics would call gullible. Others, like Robert Bly, doubt humans' ability to answer the ultimate questions and resist defining God although they will talk about "the Sacred." Robert Fulghum stresses the importance of actions over creeds.

The emerging mystics take the questions of the atheists and agnostics seriously. While orthodox religious beliefs about a personal God have inspired many people to great and noble deeds over the millennia, the image of God as a fearsome human writ large just doesn't wash any more for these writers and artists. With their intuition and the insights gained from scientists and contemporary thinkers, they are gradually shaping a new kind of mysticism. In their eclectic ways, they understand the task of both the artist and the mystic is to forge fresh metaphors to comprehend the ineffable. They are finding the universe is alive. As Findley says, "Everything is holy."

∿

Although these writers and artists fall into four loose groupings, it would be a mistake to overemphasize the categories. Whether atheist or mystic, all are bound together by a common quality: creative curiosity. They don't fret about adhering to dogmas or rigid categories of right and wrong. They bravely ask hard questions. They follow wherever their imaginative hearts and minds lead them.

When someone in this book uses the word "God," the reader has to pay attention, because not everyone means the same thing by this term. It's safe to say, however, that none of the subjects of these profiles believes in an all-controlling God who will protect them from every pain and tragedy. Almost all reject traditional beliefs about God as a being who manipulates all aspects of our life, ready to intervene to ensure everything works out for the best in the end.

Those who believe in some form of divinity think God is the ground of surprise, creativity, and adventure. In fact, the collective spirituality and philosophy of all these writers and artists fuels an astonishing creativity, requiring a courageous, compassionate commitment to an open-ended future — risky because it's not preordained. With the power of institutional religion waning, these creative people are becoming our new spiritual leaders, the unofficial priests of our era. As these brave souls wrestle with God, love, death, and beliefs that matter, may they help you see the world anew.

The Atheists

That which has been believed by everyone,
always and everywhere,
has every chance of being false.
— PAUL VALERY

Mordecai Richler

*"In a sense, all my work is about a search for values,
or a code of honor, that one can live by."*

When Mordecai Richler was a youngster, his devout, hot-tempered, paternal Jewish grandfather died. Although Richler, a budding atheist even then, had often argued bitterly with his grandfather, his mother insisted he should go to the funeral. But when Richler arrived, an uncle immediately drove him into a corner and told him he'd hastened his grandfather's death.

"I didn't bring on his death," young Richler said.

"Well, smart guy, you're the one who is mentioned first in his will."

"Oh," said Richler, surprised.

All became clear when the uncle continued, "You are not a good Jew and you are not to touch his coffin. It says so in his will. Don't you dare touch his coffin."

In his book *This Year in Jerusalem*, one of North America's greatest storytellers relates this potentially devastating vignette without personal comment. Surrounded by his cigar smoke in a Vancouver restaurant, the dishevelled Richler is only slightly more inclined to talk about the emotional price he paid for rejecting the strict Hasidic Jewish practices in which he was raised in Montreal. "I was just a kid. Fourteen I guess. So it was a bit frightening, or chilling. Although I guess I was quite defiant at the time."

Did the coffin incident help turn him off religious Judaism?

"No, no. We had disputes long before that."

When pressed, Richler acknowledges that his grandfather whipped him with a belt, grabbed his ears, and beat his face on occasion, such as the time he found out his grandson had not been observing the Sabbath. Richler gives a street-tough shrug. "He wasn't the best teacher for Orthodox practices."

In *This Year in Jerusalem*, Richler tells how, in the 1940s, as a young member of the socialist Zionist Habonim movement, he made a commitment to make *aliyah* — to emigrate to Israel. Yet when he stepped out of what he calls his "closed Jewish universe" to attend college and discovered literary geniuses such as W. B. Yeats, W. H. Auden, and Fyodor Dostoyevsky, he writes, "It was a whole world I hadn't suspected. I realized I wasn't only Jewish. And I would prefer going to Paris than Tel Aviv."

Now in his sixties, Richler still lashes out against tradition, as he has for decades in his wildly creative, internationally praised comic novels, which include *The Apprenticeship of Duddy Kravitz, Joshua Then and Now* (both of which became movies), the children's classic *Jacob Two-Two Meets the Hooded Fang,* and the epic *Solomon Gursky Was Here.* He uses humor to attack injustice and pomposity. Like a Hebrew prophet, he scolds hypocrisy and small-mindedness. But his work also has a tender side, in which a discerning conscience shines through. He stands up for his old friends and for Canada as much as for his Jewish roots. Like his famous character Duddy Kravitz, Richler is in some ways just a regular guy searching for a moral code to live by.

Although he revolted early and often against his culturally fertile but oppressively strict Hasidic upbringing, he doesn't make a big philosophical thing of it. "My initial rebellion was not very profound," he says, taking a drag from his pencil-thin black cigar. "You could even argue it was shallow. I mean, I wanted to listen to the radio on Saturday, go to baseball games, and do whatever I liked. So it was just a rebellion against the restrictions. I couldn't obey all those little sabbath laws."

Although Richler aims self-critical jokes at himself in *This Year in Jerusalem,* and is sharply insightful about conflicts within Jewish culture, he is not famous for delicate introspection. He spends only two lines in the book to say that he became an atheist: "Hardly a year after my bar mitzvah, I no longer put on phylacteries to say the morning prayers, or even attended Sabbath services. I had become an *apikoros,* an unbeliever."

Asked if he still does not believe in God, he says, "There's just one trip around the block and you better have as good a time as possible without hurting anybody else. But beyond that, that's it. Only Shirley MacLaine is guaranteed return trips again and again."

Richler maintains, as do many atheists, that religion has been mostly a force for destruction. "Through the ages, it's probable that more deadly sins have been committed in the exalted names of Jehovah,

Christ, and Allah than were ever perpetrated in the service of pride, covetousness, lust, anger, gluttony, envy, and sloth."

He refers to anti-Palestinian Orthodox Jews as "religious crazies as bad as the Ayatollahs, and as intolerant." Their undue influence in Israeli politics is resented, he says, in Israel's largely secular society. A supporter of Peace Now (a group that has influenced the treaties of the 1990s in the Middle East), Richler has long argued that both Jews and Palestinians have a right to a homeland in Israel. Although glad that Jews have the firepower to protect themselves, he admits that he finds himself hoping that if he and his friends had been born and raised in the squalor of a Palestinian settlement, "rather than the warmth of St. Urbain, we would have had the courage to be among the stone throwers."

Richler enjoys tweaking the noses of religious Zionists, poking holes in the logic used by many Jews to defend their sacred right to the territory of Israel. "The land, the biblical freehold, was given to the sons of Abraham," he says. But Hagar, Abraham's maid, also bore Abraham sons, including Ishmael, whom Genesis 21:13 says would make a great nation. Hagar and Ishmael are venerated by Arab Muslims, including many Palestinians. Thus, "arguably," he concludes, "even the biblical title to Israel is clouded."

Around Richler, everyone has to watch out; he is not of the how-to-win-friends-and-influence-people school. He is infamous for being a tough, brusque interview — quick to puncture pretension and what he considers unhealthy illusion, such as religion. Sitting with me in a noisy restaurant over breakfast, his thick, dishevelled hair falling over his left eye, he is conscientious and respectful, but not exactly ready to spill his emotional guts. He answers some questions with a blunt no, but seems to enjoy others.

He offers a clue to his irascible nature in *Solomon Gursky Was Here*, in which a mythical, magical raven keeps mysteriously showing up either to help or to laugh at the novel's characters as they make their way from obscenely expensive mansions in the East to primordial, cultic struggles in the Arctic. In the author's note to the book, Richler says he's indebted to *Raven Steals the Light*, by Bill Reid and Robert Bringhurst, for its explanation of how Haida Indians see the raven as a trickster. Perhaps this bird, with its unquenchable itch to meddle and provoke, and to play jokes on the world and its creatures, represents Richler himself.

One of Richler's tricks is to extol, despite his atheism, some of the good things about religious tradition. He appreciates Jewish culture and finds it shocking that many young people today don't read the Bible or understand its stories, pursuing melodramatic New Age sects instead. In *This Year in Jerusalem*, Richler devotes a chapter to a story written by his maternal grandfather, a prestigious rabbi who taught fear of the devil and Kabalistic mysticism. The story is about a *golem*, a Frankenstein-like creature the Jewish imagination created to fight Gentiles who persecuted them in Eastern Europe.

Also surprisingly, Richler claims he can see the attraction of Hasidism. "In an odd way, if you're a militant Orthodox Jew, it works for you," he clarifies. "It's a life full of ceremonies and holidays and a moral code. But if you don't accept it, it doesn't work. I'm very grateful for my Hasidic childhood because it was very rich in imagery and legends. But I couldn't hang with it because I found it very suffocating." He would not, on the other hand, consider replacing the Orthodox Judaism he had imposed on him as a youth with the more liberal Reform Judaism, which is increasingly popular in North America as it generally offers a nondogmatic, nonliteral route to divinity. "No, no. I believe if you're going to go to a synagogue, you go to a proper synagogue. I mean Reform is sort of like being a *Reader's Digest* Jew," he says with a quick laugh. "I don't object to it. I'm just not attracted to it."

19

Asked if any memorable passages from Jewish tradition stick with him, he cites a story about Hillel, a rabbinic sage born sixty years before Jesus, who had similar teachings. "Hillel was a great early humanist, and a great tolerant man. There used to be two schools. The school of Hillel was very humane. And the school of Shammai was very rigorous. There was a famous, probably apocryphal, story about a young Gentile who went to Shammai and asked, 'How can I become a Jew?' And Shammai said, 'Take four or five years of study. It is a difficult, arduous task.' So the Gentile then went to see Hillel and Hillel said, 'Do unto thy neighbor as you do unto yourself, and you're a Jew.'"

That's an ethical definition of Judaism that Richler can live with; it's also an approach that's increasingly attractive to the large population of secular Jews in Britain and North America. Richler retains only a few Jewish practices, such as the Passover seder. When his five adult children gather at his Quebec home, Richler and his wife, Florence, celebrate the traditional meal and drinking of wine. "We do it in a very nonreligious way, but following the rituals. It's a very moving ceremony. It's the Exodus story of Jews escaping slavery. And I like the old songs. I can still sing some of them to my children."

Richler has been married to Florence, a Gentile, for decades. When their kids were young, in Britain, they took them to synagogue a few times. "I like them to know where they came from," Richler says, "but they make their own choices." Richler mocks Jewish purists, who frown on intermarriage, by calling his five children "half-breeds." And he finds it extremely distasteful when some Jews call intermarriage the new Holocaust. None of his kids are observant, although they're interested in religion. Of the two who married, both married Jews.

"I could imagine some people finding Jews quite tiresome," he comments. He is interrupted by a coughing jag, then continues. "For years they were objecting because they weren't being accepted, and now they're screaming because their children are intermarrying, which is inevitable as people become integrated into society. I think all cultures enrich each other." Jewish culture, he states, will live on — even though it is only six million strong on a continent of 280 million Gentiles.

"If the only possible strength for the survival of Jewish culture is anti-Semitism, then it would be a very pathetic tradition. And I don't think that's the case at all. Anti-Semitism isn't necessary for its survival. That would be a confession of inadequacy if it were. I would consider it legitimate among actual survivors of the Holocaust to be anxious about everything. But we've had a very soft life here. And I think it's paranoid to be worried about a Gentile threat. Jews have entered into the mainstream."

Some Jews wish Richler would just shut up and keep his criticism of Jews to Jewish circles — protect the fort at all costs. "But my case has always been anti-Semites don't need ammunition. And if you were going to take them into consideration every time you wrote something, it would be a form of censorship and a kind of triumph for them."

Some pillars of the Jewish community have never forgiven him for writing the acclaimed *Apprenticeship of Duddy Kravitz* (published in 1959). He laughs uproariously when asked why they thought it offensive. "That's a good question. Part of the problem is it was read by a number of people who'd never read modern serious fiction. The larger Jewish community tends to confuse its writers with the anti-defamation league. But there's a long tradition, going all the way back to biblical times, of Jews being very critical of their own society." Another problem, he says, is that some Jews interpreted Duddy Kravitz as a metaphor for all of North American Jewry. But he was just a character typical of the Montreal friends Richler grew up with: a provincial kid with his eye on the main chance.

Richler has a lot of affection for Kravitz, the same way he does for the old friends he follows in *This Year in Jerusalem*, including a socialist who did make *aliyah* to Israel and still lives on a kibbutz. As for his own principles, Richler now considers himself part social democrat, part conservative. "I subscribe to social democratic ideas about taxation, and getting on to the rich, and so on. But some of their political correctness irritates the hell out of me."

Like Duddy Kravitz, indeed like most of the protagonists in his novels, Richler paints himself as a guy searching for an identity and a moral guide. Asked where his values come from, the leather-skinned novelist takes another drag on his cigar and seems to look within himself for an authentic answer.

"In a sense, all my work is about a search for values, or a code of honor, that one can live by. You know that famous phrase of Dostoyevsky's: 'If God is dead, then everything is legal.' Well, I don't think everything is legal if God is dead. Humanists assume more responsibility for their own conduct, for what they do. I think it's very important to not commit antisocial acts, or exploit other people or do bad things."

Richler seems content with the definition of himself he has outlined: as a writer and humorist who pricks pretension; as a secular humanist who does what's right for its own sake, not because he fears God's punishment; and a Jew who intends to keep identifying himself as a Jew, despite watching baseball on the Sabbath. One guesses he will stick to it for the rest of his days.

"Once every four or five years, I might wander by a synagogue. And of course there's a certain nostalgia because I remember singing those prayers myself. But we all have nostalgia for our childhood. So it's not really meaningful. I don't really yearn for it. I don't think in my declining years I'm going to enter the rabbinate."

W. P. Kinsella

"The only thing I hold against my dad . . . is that he was an atheist until he found out he was dying. Then he turned into a major coward, and went back to the Catholic fold."

W. P. (Bill) Kinsella bears no resemblance to his whimsical Iowa farmer who imagines long-dead baseball players back to life in *Shoeless Joe* (which became the hit movie *Field of Dreams*). Nor is he cut from the same cloth as the likeable character Silas Ermineskin, who narrates Kinsella's compassionate, mythological stories about Indian life.

Far from being a warm, romantic, spiritual dreamer, Kinsella is an aloof, cynical, irreverent, contradictory atheist with a chip on his shoulder. A die-hard individualist, he fights for law and order and campaigns for right-wing causes. And he wears cowboy clothes.

In other words, he's an interesting and disturbing guy to spend an afternoon with, partly at his home and partly over lunch at Tim Horton's donut shop, where we walk to calm his growling, diabetic stomach.

Like the refreshing spring breeze wafting over the beach near his home in White Rock, a cliff-hugging West Coast town just minutes north of the U.S. border, Kinsella's best-selling stories are filled with tender metaphor, gentle characters, and uplifting ideals. In most of his fifteen novels and two hundred short stories, Kinsella paints a mystical, community-oriented, sentiment-drenched world.

Now entering his sixties, he says he writes the way he does because he's an "entertainer." Ever since he was five years old, Kinsella has been hooked by the life of the imagination. He gives readers what they want, which is attractive protagonists and upbeat endings. "I want readers to feel warm and fuzzy, and leave them with a little tear in the eye."

He floods his fiction with religious imagery because it's fun and it sells. "Weird stuff is entertaining," he says, eyes glinting hard under his cowboy hat, "and academics derive sexual stimulation from it." He adds, caustically, that "in another life, if I knew what I know now, I'd get into TV evangelism. Because TV evangelism proves you obviously don't have to believe any of what you say to be successful."

Kinsella is certainly successful. His books have sold more than two million copies. He makes roughly $170,000 a year. He sold the rights to *Shoeless Joe* for $250,000. Norman Jewison produced a movie based on *Dance Me Outside*, which was directed by Bruce McDonald, and formed the basis for a Canadian TV series in 1996. Kinsella keeps houses in both British Columbia and Palm Springs, California, where he spends the winter.

He is also a devilishly good writer. He's won international critical acclaim and many awards, including the Stephen Leacock Medal for Humour for *The Fencepost Chronicles*. He's the only Canadian to win the prestigious Houghton-Mifflin Literary Award, and is a member of the Order of Canada.

The house he has just built on a cul-de-sac is big but ordinary, with light blue vinyl siding and a drab fragment of front lawn. "I keep to myself," he says, "and expect my neighbors to do the same." His second-floor office, with its huge dining-room table in the middle for a desk, is decorated with baseballs, promotional posters of his books, and portraits of himself. Sitting under a small window that looks out on a few evergreen trees and neighboring houses, Kinsella launches into a tirade that debunks any myths about him being a softie — especially when it comes to religion.

"I think the church is a vile organization. The Catholic Church is as evil as any organization that exists in the world. Fundamentalists and Catholics operate solely on fear and guilt. Most wars are religiously inspired. Fundamentalists say, 'Do it my way or I'll kill you.' They think they're better because they're going to heaven. My view is freedom of religion also means freedom *from* religion."

Kinsella donates at least $1,000 a year to the American Atheists, a group headed by the controversial Madalyn Murray O'Hair, who led the 1960s Supreme Court challenge that effectively killed prayer and Bible readings in American public schools. Kinsella is determined to keep up the battle against school prayer.

He is like O'Hair in many ways. He is religiously antireligious. He prides himself on ticking people off. There is a reckless courage about him; he doesn't care if he appears to be a bigot. Yet in his contrary way, he is a moral purist.

But what about the miracle in *Shoeless Joe* of the deceased White Sox players who allegedly threw the 1919 World Series walking out of the cornfields to reconcile themselves and play again? Is there any possibility Kinsella believes in an afterlife?

"I certainly don't," he says, staring, making sure the point is not missed. "It's just the same as when you squish an ant on the sidewalk. No one thinks ants go to ant heaven. It's sheer hubris — that we would have the gall to think there's an afterlife for creatures like us."

The death of Kinsella's father caused one of Kinsella's biggest disappointments in life. "The only thing I hold against my dad, a lapsed Catholic, is that he was an atheist until he found out he was dying. Then he turned into a major coward, and went back to the Catholic fold. I guess he was playing the odds, just in case."

Kinsella also believes his father, a semipro baseball player and farmer, was too soft to be financially successful.

Kinsella, on the other hand, with his curled moustache, turquoise jewelry, and hat covering his thin, long hair, is determined not to be pushed around by Catholicism, or the world. "I've always had a chip on my shoulder when it comes to taking orders from anyone," he says. "That's also the way I raised my two daughters. I'd tell them, 'Anything you choose to do, you can do. You have to have stamina and be persistent and not take any crap from anybody.'" He's proud of his daughters, both of whom are now in their thirties. Erin is raising three children while holding down a newspaper route; Shannon manages a construction company.

Although Kinsella claims to have no interest in religion or even philosophy, his life, paradoxically, is governed by a rock-hard philosophical principle: that individual rights and freedoms reign supreme. "I don't care if people worship blue frogs," he says, "as long as they don't push it on me. I don't like to be told what to do."

He's near-maniacal about his conviction that no government, no boss, no interest group, NOBODY, has the right to force him to do anything. "I have no patience with people who disrupt people's lives to change the system. I don't carry a gun, but if some protesters tried to block my car during a demonstration, I'd probably go berserk and shoot them," he says, a steely edge entering his voice. And despite the criticism that has been aimed at him for writing from a native Indian point of view, he insists novelists should have the liberty to appropriate the voice of anybody they please.

Kinsella's rugged, combative individualism is in part a reaction to his father's soft-heartedness. "He was good-natured, probably too much so. He was too proud to take welfare when the Depression came along. He bought this worthless piece of land in Alberta. We just existed. He would hire people because they needed work, rather than get good workers. They'd work two days and then they'd be gone. We'd never see them again, except when they needed a job."

When his father died, his mother had just $300 in the bank. She eventually managed to make a large profit in real estate. "She was capable financially, which Dad never was."

Kinsella's loner tendencies began in childhood where, an only child on an isolated farm in northern Alberta, he was home-schooled by his mother. He had no friends but created a rich imaginary life for his cat and toys. At the age of eleven, he attended school for the first time in Edmonton, where he endured cruelty from the other kids. "I learned to be tough. I'll be as mean as I have to be to critics or the bank or the post office or any bureaucrat who fucks me over," he states firmly, casually cutting his fingernails with a big pair of scissors. "But with my family and friends, I'm not cantankerous. I think my daughters would say I'm a gentle person."

His disdain for social sensibilities was further heightened during twenty-five years of "banging his head against the wall of the North

American literary establishment" until publishers finally decided they liked his work. During this time, Kinsella earned a B.A. at the University of Victoria and an M.F.A. at the University of Iowa in 1978. He taught creative writing at the University of Calgary until 1983. His academic experience left him with a loathing of university faculty and administrations. "They were worried that I didn't do research. I had the mistaken idea that having a Ph.D. and a teaching position would make people less petty than the average idiot. There were four or five knives in my back. I learned not to take any crap. A lot of being successful in any field is being able to say 'I told you so, you son of a bitch. Look at me now.'"

Kinsella calls himself liberal (meaning pro-individual rights) on women's equality and abortion, but conservative on everything else. "I'm very much law and order. I think thugs have no rights — I'd cut wasteful government programs, which is most of them." He supports free trade. His pet peeves include unions, the CBC, bilingualism, seat belts, and Greenpeace.

He continues to thumb his nose at North America's literary and artistic community, which includes many progressive-minded people, by boldly venturing into right-wing politics. He campaigned for the Reform Party of Canada in the 1993 federal election. The voice of the Reform TV and radio commercials was Kinsella's — and many of them featured a twist on the line "If you build it, he will come," which became a widely quoted aphorism after the success of *Field of Dreams*. The line was changed in the ads to: "If you come, we will build it."

But there's an apparent contradiction with Kinsella being a dyed-in-the-wool acolyte of the Reform Party, which is ideologically similar to the Republican Party in the United States. The Republican Party is heavily influenced by evangelical Christians, and Reform leader Preston Manning *is* an evangelical Christian. What gives?

Kinsella would prefer Manning wasn't evangelical, but he can tolerate it. "He's made every effort to keep church and state separate. And he doesn't force his religious views on others."

Even though Kinsella claims that 90 percent of people in power are incompetent, he won't join fellow novelists such as Mordecai Richler, Timothy Findley, and John Irving and inject social critique into his writing. "I'm just a storyteller. I'm not trying to change anybody's point of view." He consciously avoids insinuating his values into his work, other than to occasionally lampoon evangelical Christians, as he does in *The Dixon Cornbelt League*.

What does all this say about atheism, or at least this particular atheist? Does it say, "Without God, everything is permitted?" Does it say that, without some overarching, transcendent guide, art will inevitably give way to the marketplace and making a buck? It is a tempting analysis, but it doesn't quite hit the mark. Anyone who writes as sensitively as Kinsella does, with such an understanding of the heart's desire for larger meaning, can't be completely unfeeling and indifferent. And he is not a phony. If he were, he wouldn't bother telling me about his strict atheism. He would let the world have its wishful view of him as a warm-hearted mystic. It would sell more books. Instead, Kinsella revels in disillusioning his followers, especially academics. "I like," he says, "to be able to laugh at people who take my work seriously."

Another paradox, more surprising, emerges near the end of our time together. Kinsella reveals that his third wife, poet Ann Knight, is a Christian, albeit, "a moderate Christian." She attends the Anglican Church. They don't discuss her religion.

They have since separated.

Bill Reid

"Raven is the force that keeps the world turning. Raven is a demigod who does things inadvertently. He goes through eternity turning over rocks to see what's underneath."

When he dies, Bill Reid, the creator of some of the world's most famous works of native art, wants his Haida sculptor friend, Gary Edenshaw, to haul his body onto a boat, weigh it down with a heavy chain, and drop it to a sandy West Coast ocean bottom to become food for crabs. Three days later Reid would like his friends to hold a party at the same beach and feast on the crabs that ate his body.

Reid's nontraditional funeral plans make it clear that he does not buy into Haida religion. This may shock and disappoint many people who have been drawn by Reid's wondrous mythological creatures to the spirituality of indigenous people. In his seventies, frail from old age and shaking from Parkinson's disease, Reid dreamed up his burial ritual in part because he doesn't accept the Haida belief in reincarnation, especially the notion that souls of high-ranking Haida will temporarily inhabit the body of another animal, such as a dog, before being reborn as a human. He is not fond of dogs.

Reid is a cheerful debunker. "Life is very short and man has little therein, save the brief loan of his own body. But that body is capable of many curious pleasures," he says, quoting the late American novelist James Branch Cabell. Although Parkinson's has made his face swollen and mask like, he manages a smile. When death comes, Reid doesn't believe he'll go to a life beyond this one. "The universe we live in is so completely enthralling and exciting in the way it works itself out, one cog meshing with another. This world is much greater than anything man can imagine. There is no need to plaster religious illusion over it," he says.

The worldview that comes out of his mouth, influenced by both Western intellectual tradition and native ways, is as bold as his powerful sculptures, which include the renowned *Spirit of Haida Gwaii*, a $1.5-million canoe packed with mythological Haida creatures that sits in the Canadian Embassy in Washington, D.C.

Reid, the product of a Haida mother and a white father, is credited with leading a renaissance in West Coast native art — and indirectly creating a global fascination with native spirituality. The renowned French anthropologist Claude Lévi-Strauss says Reid "brought Northwest art to the world scene, into dialogue with the whole of mankind." Michael Ames, the director of the University of British Columbia's Museum of Anthropology, says Reid not only initiated a resurgence of

Northwest coast native art about thirty years ago, "but is widely acclaimed as one of the greatest living native artists and one of Canada's most important sculptors, white or Indian."

Nevertheless, Reid has an uneasy relationship with the original inhabitants of the rugged Queen Charlotte Islands (known to natives as Haida Gwaii). Reid thinks most Haida lack discipline. "And I'm old enough to say what I feel like and get away with it. There has to be some advantage to getting old. You certainly don't get any respect from the people around you," he jokes, with a nod to two female assistants.

The steadier hands of these trusted assistants now finish off the ornate designs he roughs out. His artwork — a bronze human-sized statue of an orca frozen in mid-leap, some convoluted paintings, and several serigraphs spread out on the carpet — is scattered throughout his large apartment in the Kitsilano neighborhood of Vancouver.

Reid also accuses white people of romanticizing native religion, assuming all North American natives believe in a Great Spirit. But Reid doesn't believe in any God. "I believe in chance."

He quotes the late French existentialist Albert Camus: "You must learn to live without hope, but conduct your life as if there were hope." Although he never attended university, Reid is extremely well read and holds seven honorary university degrees. Assistant Jill Weidman says he can recite poetry for hours.

Reid's body has been wracked with tics and convulsions for twenty years. Because of the painful drain of his Parkinson's, his tough-minded opinions come out in a whispery voice that can be drowned out by something as insignificant as an assistant rustling paper. The apartment contains further reminders of his illness: a wheelchair, and a cane resting in a corner.

Beyond this, his rooms are a befuddling mix of styles reflecting the conflicting cultures he's found himself in since day one. Refined neo-classical paintings with baroque frames hang beside wild native masks over French colonial sofas.

Reid was raised in the B.C. wilderness by a Scots-German-American father and a Haida mother. "I lived among mountains that were 7,000 feet high. It would have been a wonderful way to grow up, but I didn't get along well with my parents. My father was a small-time entrepreneur and never liked me. He predicted nothing but continual failure for me. They were all quite nuts, my family. My mother was completely insane, although she was a beautiful designer. I was brought up completely by accident."

As a boy, the only good thing he got from forced attendance at a Protestant church was the twenty cents he stole out of the quarter his parents gave him for the collection plate. "I used the money to buy Western magazines."

Today, he still thinks little, either good or bad, about Jesus Christ, but objects to the churches' heavy-handed moral condemnations of such things as extramarital affairs because they "don't take into account natural biological urges."

Reid's one precious legacy from his childhood is a love of the wilderness, of the way nature fits together. Although it's wonderful to be human, he says with a sly smile, "life, in the end, is just a big cosmic joke. And humans, at their worst, are a sickness upon an otherwise wonderful Earth. To quote myself, 'We've made a pasture out of forest, and a desert out of pasture.'"

Virtually all Reid's work now revolves around the creatures of Haida myth, such as the eagle, bear, dogfish, salmon, and raven. The stunning *Raven and the First Man*, for example, a giant wooden sculpture at Vancouver's Museum of Anthropology, illustrates a Haida myth about Raven unlocking the first humans from a clamshell. Sounding like an anthropologist (the profession of his third wife,

Martine), Reid explains that myths are humans' attempt to make sense of a chaotic, threatening universe.

Take, for example, the personified trickster figure of raven, he says. "Raven is the force that keeps the world turning. Raven is a demigod who does things inadvertently. He goes through eternity turning over rocks to see what's underneath." In Haida myth, raven created the sun and stars while in the act of theft. Raven's antics change and reorder the world.

Many believe the trickster, the transforming principle in life, represents the surprising quality of divinity. But as an atheist, Reid, who collaborated with Robert Bringhurst on a book about the trickster figure called *Raven Steals the Light*, finds such comments meaningless. For him, the "attractive, troublesome, and quarrelsome" raven simply reflects human nature and the qualities of creativity, exemplifying the kind of creative curiosity "that has led people into more new circumstances than any other character trait."

Reid has been iconoclastic all his life. He developed an early career as a CBC broadcaster because he had a rich voice. But he failed to make much money, so he took up jewelry making on the side. He began focusing on native art more than forty years ago after discovering some long-lost Haida relatives. He recognized that Haida carving was as good, in its own way, as any other great school of classical art, and had the discipline and work ethic to follow through on his insight.

Although offered membership in the Order of Canada, Reid refused in protest against the federal government's chronic mistreatment of natives, on which he blames incredibly high rates of alcoholism, suicide, and incarceration. "Things are pretty critical for the Haida and all natives right now. They could either go ahead, or fall back," he says.

He doesn't hold the Haida blameless, however, accusing them of a tendency toward arrogance and self-righteousness. As a result, some

Haida love him, some don't. He shrugs it off; "The Haida live their lives, I live mine."

Nevertheless, Reid respects the old Haida life: "Their system of art is unique and it's absolutely unbelievable they could have begun it all in small, hunting, fishing communities. Their abstract designs of whales are as good as the real thing. I think there was enough genius in their work to find a common thread with other people."

But, ultimately, at an existential level, Reid sees West Coast artistic creations as no more than "silly geometric designs." With a devilish grin, he insists, "I would trade the whole of Haida art for the Mozart horn concertos."

Jane Rule

*"I think love is the obligation you have
to give relationships meaning."*

After Jane Rule agreed I could take the ferry over to see her on
Galiano Island, off the coast of British Columbia, I had a dream. In it,
one side of the famous author's face was normal, but the other was
raw and misshapen. Her pastoral surroundings, by contrast, were
unbelievably beautiful: green and warm, with kids joyfully splashing
in a pool.

I interpreted her disfigurement as a symbol of the stigma some attach to Rule's homosexuality, and the lush setting as symbolic of the healing refuge she sought from being seen as a freak.

When I cruise over to Rule's house a week later, only some of the dream turns out to be true. Rule does have a sun-dappled pool nestled among the trees. And island children often do play in it.

But Rule did not leave Vancouver in the mid-seventies for Galiano Island with her partner of almost forty years, Helen Sonthoff, because of discrimination. She left teaching at the University of British Columbia because she had too many friends; she was going out almost every night. There was no peace. And she needed to write. This pastoral island between Vancouver Island and Vancouver, with just a few thousand people sprinkled along its nineteen-mile length, has helped give her life some serenity — a quality which she values greatly.

When Rule answers the door of her pleasant, wooden home among the trees, her legs and hands are shaking with severe arthritis. She can barely walk. Now in her sixties and ill, she explains that she hasn't the energy to write any more books. The public will have to be satisfied with articles and short stories — and the twelve frank, caring, gently iconoclastic, wise books she has already written, all of which are still in print, many in foreign languages.

Rule's first novel, *Desert of the Heart*, became a successful movie of the same name starring Helen Shaver. Her last book, 1987's *Memory Board*, about elderly people and senility, not only brought her rave reviews, but prompted the Canadian Medical Association to ask her to speak at a national conference on Alzheimer's disease. The last few years have also brought an honorary degree from the University of British Columbia and a documentary film about her life, *Fiction and Other Truths*, that won a Canadian Genie award in 1996.

We sit down in front of her large living-room window, from which it's possible to glimpse the Vancouver–Victoria ferry maneuvering

Active Pass, not to mention observe bald-headed eagles (she counted eighteen just the day before).

"I'm a non-believer," she says bluntly, making sure she gets off on an honest foot. "I don't believe in the existence of a God. I don't believe in the Christian dogma. I find it horrifyingly silly. The intolerance that flows from organized religion is the most dangerous thing on the planet." She lost her religious faith long before people began sending her evangelical comic-book tracts condemning her lesbian existence as a living example of why God destroyed Sodom and Gomorrah. At age four, she told the teachers at her religious nursery that "Santa Claus was better than God because Santa Claus brought presents." She was punished for her candor by being confined to a school closet. Then, to top it all off, someone told her Santa Claus wasn't real — and neither were the Easter Bunny and the Tooth Fairy. That was it for little Jane. "I think I thought that since all those things were a hoax, God must be too."

Although Rule minored in comparative religion at Mills College in California and keeps a Bible on the writing desk in her book-filled office off the pool patio, it's only because she's "fearfully interested in the power of organized religion." Rule's close friends, however, include an Episcopalian nun from Seattle, a female Anglican deacon on Galiano, and a few gays in the United Church of Canada. More than once, people have told her her ethics, and sense of justice seem awfully close to those of Christians or Jews, albeit the liberal variety.

Rule's lifestyle is not exactly what most politically conservative proponents of the "family-values movement" mean by the term, but family values is exactly what Rule's work explores. Rule's stories focus on home life: child-bearing, marriage, affairs, death, relatives, vulnerability, friends, growth, separation, acceptance of differences, aging. The presence of some gay characters creates surprising, sometimes challenging, climaxes. Her book *Inland Passage* includes a short story titled "The Real World," about a grandmother coming to terms with her granddaughter's sexuality. The title sums up Rule's searingly honest approach to reality. The title of her book of essays also provides a wonderful label for her: *A Hot-Eyed Moderate*.

But from what source do Rule's passionate purpose and ethics radiate, if not, as they do for many, from belief in an all-loving higher power? Lighting a cigarette, she replies, "It seems to me odd to require a force other than ourselves to make our life meaningful. I think what I believe is people have to invest meaning in life." The easiest way to do that is to be a novelist, she says, because you're creating meaning with every word. But literature is not the only way to live an authentic life. "I think you're doing your job just by living every day, paying real attention, however you do that. Any kind of concerted attention is valuable."

Book reviewers from New York to Munich have noted that the overriding qualities in Rule's work are compassion and honesty. Many of her stories focus on the simple pleasures of home life and the difficulties of raising children in a materialistic world. The *Toronto Star* said, "Her great strength is that people carry on, life has meaning, love is important. Rule's fiction feels like a pillar one leans on to gain strength."

Rule is refreshing in the way she rejects convoluted fiction designed mainly to show off the genius of the writer. "A work of art is not a clever puzzle to be solved by clever readers," she once told a literary journal. "It is a passionately articulated vision to be gently shared."

To Rule, work of all kinds is important, particularly when it's done to accomplish something more than pay the mortgage, and women who have been able to spend their time raising children "are enormously lucky."

Her own purposefulness in life comes from a sense of justice and gratitude. "I think of just being born as a colossal win," she says, even while her hands shake. "I think it's an extraordinary accident we should make use of. We're especially fortunate to be born into this culture and language. None of us has any business being unhappy. The quality of how people live lives matters to me."

Rule believes that although many people, including her, often hide from their duties, everyone needs to be responsible "to the environment, to the political realm, and to the suffering of so much of the world." Every minute she speaks, her initial description of herself as a "non-believer" seems more ironic; Rule obviously believes in many overriding, universal values, far more than the typical churchgoer or half-hearted person of faith.

Robertson Davies said disillusionment is the source of the atheism of many romantic people. But Rule isn't disillusioned with the world; she is dedicated to it and attentive to its needs. "I've been interested in the stewardship of what money I've had," she says. She gives low-interest loans to islanders who want to invest in homes or small businesses. She donates to various civil liberties associations, Amnesty International, women's organizations, and groups dedicated to the conservation of Mount Galiano, among other causes.

Rule attributes her compassion to growing up an outsider. Although she moved to Canada in 1956, she was raised in Plainfield, New York, by parents who were married for sixty-five years in a "wonderful relationship." She felt different, however, even before she knew she was a lesbian. She just had a way of speaking out, as her comments on Santa Claus and God attest, that isolated her. That's why she watches out for cliquishness among the island children, whose company she generally delights in; until the onset of arthritis in the early 1990s, she often acted as lifeguard or gave swimming lessons. "I'm very fierce about making sure the kids don't torment each other."

Rule objects to members of minorities — gays, feminists, Christians, or anyone — who act superior because of their outsider status. "It's a defence. It's a sorrow to see a minority ape the worst of the majority." The crucial thing is to nurture bonds wherever they arise, she says. Rule has always been close to her family, and she values the many friends that have popped into her life as if by accident.

"I'm bothered by the idea that you choose who you love," she says. "I didn't choose my relatives or the kids who come here. My nephew is a big macho man with huge shoulders. I tell him: 'You're the oddest person to be given to me to love.' And I adore him. I think love is the obligation you have to give relationships meaning."

A nasty cough rumbles deep inside her, a legacy of fifty years of smoking. She wishes she wasn't addicted, but she's beyond fighting it.

"I have no ambition to live to a great age. I think old age is the pits. I've seen it. To outlive your usefulness is not to me a great thing." She doesn't fear death, which she considers to be just nothingness. In fact, she says, "the only thing I don't like about death is that other people do it. I would like to pass a law that no one I love is allowed to die."

When her eighty-eight-year-old father died in 1993 on Galiano, Rule felt angry. "Most of grief is self-pity," she admits. But she genuinely missed his goodness, a quality which seemed to embarrass him. "I think in our society a lot of people are ashamed of good motives. My father was close to ashamed of his own beauty, his own generosity, his kindness. Yet a lot of people yearn for that kind of purpose."

At the end of the day, I drive back to the island's ferry terminal, where I end up conversing with a long-haired Galiano Island carpenter. He tells me about a single parent who had never met Rule before but had just gone to see her about a mortgage. She got it. With my dream images now out of the way, the memory left of Rule is of real compassion, real responsibility, real purpose. "The Real World."

Robert Munsch

*"I find the whole pageant of
life and evolution just wonderful."*

Sitting in his big brick house at the end of a cul-de-sac in Guelph, Ontario, his black standard poodle lying at his sneaker-clad feet, Robert Munsch explains that he wrote his most famous children's book, *Love You Forever*, while grieving for his babies who were born dead. Performing in front of thousands of children, Munsch is a paragon of goofiness. Most of his children's books are outrageous fun, though marbled with messages. But as with many comics, you wonder whether, if Munsch wasn't laughing so much, maybe he'd be crying.

Love You Forever recounts a mother's and son's vows of eternal devotion as they move through their lives toward death. It has sold more than seven million copies in North America, and the *New York Times* has named it North America's top-selling book for young children. "People like it," he says, "because it integrates death into life."

It's hard to hear Munsch talk about his little book without feeling the intensity of the sorrow and depression he suffered two decades ago when his wife gave birth to two stillborn children in a row. Munsch speaks about the deaths with the calm perspective of a man who has worked it through. "The book is what would have happened if the kids grew up," he says. "The book is my monument to my kids." He and his wife, as one way of coping with the pain of grief, used to sing the tender refrain that became the heart of *Love You Forever*. "I'll love you forever/I'll like you for always." Munsch especially appreciates it when parents whose children have also died have told him how much they value the book.

He himself has found a perspective on the agony over his dead children through emotional honesty and a brave-minded worldview. Munsch realized the babies died simply because he and his wife had a problem transmitting genes.

Did their deaths influence his beliefs about God? "My brief answer is, I'm an atheist," he says. He thought about God a lot during his grief, and indeed his loss of faith was partly a result of the question "What kind of God would allow two children to die?"

"I'm not saying there isn't a God," he says. Then he adds quietly, with an almost offhand dart of anger, "But there isn't a God who cares about people. And who wants a God who doesn't give a shit?"

Although he stopped believing in God after the death of his children, Munsch had begun questioning Christianity much earlier. In

1971, he decided to end seven years of training for the priesthood.

Raised in Pittsburgh, Pennsylvania, in a family of nine children, he had entered a Jesuit seminary mainly because his Catholic parents expected it. "My older brother was the family hood, so I became the family saint." He joined a group of counterculture, antiwar Jesuits working in inner-city Boston. While preparing for the priesthood, however, he also studied anthropology at Boston University. "Anthropology is about the relativity of all belief systems," he says. "I guess the anthropology won."

Munsch found that the idea that no single worldview could claim the corner on truth clashed with the church's demand that he buy the orthodox Catholic package. "It was presented as you eat the whole pizza or nothing at all." His studies in anthropology led him to question the Vatican doctrine that proclaimed the Pope infallible, artificial birth control sinful, and eternal salvation available through Christ alone. Some of his colleagues training for the priesthood took vows even though they didn't buy the package, hoping the church would eventually reform. But not Munsch. "I didn't want to lie to people."

He left the seminary at age twenty-five, but with no hard feelings against the Jesuits, whom he calls "amazing and wonderful people." He is still in contact with some of them. He began working in day cares in tough neighborhoods in Boston and New York, where, to quiet the children, he learned his renowned knack for telling tall tales.

On stage, he's rather like Robin Williams, a ball of exploding energy. But in his book-filled basement in this pleasant town of old brick buildings, wide streets, shopping malls, and pizza parlors, where he emigrated nineteen years ago from the Eastern United States, Munsch is soft-spoken and almost shy. An articulate sensitivity shines through. He is a caring man, a kind of atheist mystic. If the Catholic doctrine had held, one senses he could have been a good priest.

Instead he married, and eventually adopted three children.

Munsch now has about twenty children's books in print. His works have been translated into eleven languages, including Chinese, and have sold more than fifteen million copies in total. He is the third-best-selling children's author alive, outranked only by Jan and Stan Berenstain and Mercer Meyer.

Although his irreverent books aim mainly to amuse kids (and parents), Munsch believes they have a general theme: that people can get along, even if they fight a lot. "It's something I've had to learn. My family had the Irish handling of anger; you didn't raise your voice. My books are about how it's okay to argue and disagree. Eventually things work out." *Love You Forever*, for example, captures the primal bond parents feel even for children who drive them crazy. The book is about how "people are the only show in town. If you can't value and love people, you're failing."

In many other Munsch books, such as *Thomas's Snowsuit*, authority figures (in the shape of school principals, or parents, mayors, or technology), have their noses affectionately tweaked. It's been said that anyone raised by Jesuits either ends up obedient or a rebel; it's not hard to imagine that characters such as the bumbling mayor in *Jonathan Cleaned Up, Then He Heard a Sound* was inspired by an old church official who tried to keep young Munsch in line.

In the delightfully rude books, *Good Families Don't* and *I Have to Go!*, Munsch teaches kids that their bodies are okay with tales about farting and peeing. "I grew up a good, repressed Catholic — the world, the flesh, and the devil," he says with a smile. "It really mucked up my sex life. I had a bad body image. It took me a long time to realize I didn't have to be a saint — I could just be a human being. It's good to be a human being."

His feminist views come forward in *Angela's Airplane* and his second most popular book, *The Paper Bag Princess* (three million copies sold), where the princess decides, for the first time in legend history, not to marry the prince. Some day, without making a big deal of it, Munsch plans to quietly insert two lesbian parents into a book.

Munsch and his family attended the non-doctrinaire Unitarian church in Guelph until the routine petered out, mainly because his kids grew restless. He approves of the way churches get people involved in local ethical issues. He gave money to charities before he had any real money to give away; now, he says, "I give to too many charities" — everything from the Ontario Naturalists to Canadian Save the Children.

Now in his fifties, Munsch still writes to his Jesuit friends, and still feels fondly toward Catholicism. When the Pope announced that Catholics should stop talking about even the possibility of ordaining women, for example, Munsch says it was like hearing someone you like saying something you don't like. "You say: 'Oh, why did he say that?'"

Munsch misses the certainty of belief that Catholicism provided — "all the answers to all the important questions." But he definitely doesn't miss "the Catholic emphasis on guilt and redemption."

For his current cosmology, Munsch looks to the stars. At night, he frequently takes his telescope out in front of his home, where a broken street-hockey net sits under fluttering maples. "My daughter," he says, "would often ask me why I spend so much time peering into space. I didn't know what to tell her at first. Then I finally said, 'I like to see how big things are and how small I am.' I find the whole dance of the universe — from stars to DNA — amazing. I don't know what it's for. But I find the whole pageant of life and evolution just wonderful."

While he was in the seminary, Munsch devoured the works of the late Jesuit theologian and paleontologist Pierre Teilhard de Chardin. Embraced today by a wide variety of seekers who have rejected ortho-dox religion, Teilhard de Chardin tried to emphasize how divinity was part of the evolutionary process. (Teilhard de Chardin says God cannot stop all suffering, but suffers empathetically when humans and others feel pain.) But the books and magazines that line Munsch's basement — including *The Faith Healers*, by James Randi, who makes a career out of debunking claims about miracles or paranormal experiences, and titles by Harvard University biologist Stephen Jay Gould, who criticizes Teilhard de Chardin's theories — provide testament to Munsch's current rejection of almost all aspects of a divine worldview.

He pulls out one of his favorite books from the floor-to-ceiling shelves. *Five Kingdoms: An Illustrated Guide to the Phyla of Life on Earth* is hard-core microscopic biology, about single-cell creatures and the evolutionary process. Munsch devours such stuff. He'll stare at a glass of water, or a leaf, marveling and wondering. "The totally mind-boggling complexity of things," he says, "is bizarre and humbling." While some theologians say the ordering principle behind this complexity is God, Munsch will only allow that they're free to call it that. He himself won't.

The only book he's published in which a God figure appears is *Giant: Waiting for the Thursday Boat*, which was banned in one Ontario school district. It's about a cosmic battle between a pagan giant and a Christian, St. Patrick. For Munsch, it's an allegory about accepting differences. "It's a very personal story for me. The thing that always amazed me about my family was that we got along, even though we have a monk in the family, and good Catholics and lukewarm Catholics and people like me and people who are more extreme atheists than me."

Giant portrays God as a little girl. While some conservative Christians hated the book, many liberal Christians loved its portrayal of God as an easygoing peacemaker rather than a fearsome omnipotent being. It better fit their idea of how Jesus embodied divinity. If God existed,

Munsch feels God would be much more likely to be manifested in a tiny kid than in a powerful figure. But the main reason he portrayed the divinity as a girl in *Giant* was his daughter's complaint that God is usually portrayed as male. "You write books. You can make God whatever you want," she told him, showing an intuitive awareness of the myth-making power of the imagination.

Munsch was hard to categorize for this book. He won't use the word "God," but will talk about "the transcendent" — the sense of something greater he feels when he gazes at the stars or at the veins of a leaf. Although his atheism is sensitive and in some ways similar to a mystical worldview, Munsch refuses to accept the teaching of even cutting-edge Christians such as Teilhard de Chardin who say God is part of the natural world; the entity that lures the world toward growth and evolution. And he definitely rejects the God of orthodox theologians, who is expected to make everything — from the war in the former Yugoslavia to the death of a child — "turn out for the best."

Like many who grew up on the standard church theology of an Almighty God who is supposed to control everything in the universe, Munsch is now mistrustful of all theology. He believes he gains more realistic, if less comforting, insights from the pure scientific study of nature. "The enormous dance of life and evolution gives answers — although they're not always nice answers," he says. One "not-nice" reality he believes nature has forced him to face is that his children did not go to an afterlife. "When you're dead, you're dead. Your disk is wiped clean."

He finds it comical when people try to tell him that, as a big-time author, he's now immortal. How can an author, let alone a kids' author, become immortal? "In the scheme of things, the English language isn't immortal," he says. "The Earth isn't immortal." In the dance of life, even his precious stars will eventually die.

The
Doubters

Modest doubt is the beacon of the wise.
— WILLIAM SHAKESPEARE

John Irving

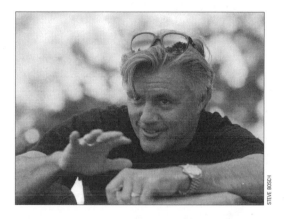

"It doesn't seem to me that doubt is the opposite of faith.
Doubt is an integral part of faith."

Unlike most people, John Irving had the benefit of a solid, liberal Christian education. Because of this background, Irving, one of North America's most celebrated novelists, continues to take Christianity — and other religions — seriously. He is still eager to mine the wisdom in Judeo-Christian thought, even though many in today's intelligentsia have written it off. His interest in religion shows up in *The World According to Garp*; it is central to *A Prayer for Owen Meany* and plays a role in *A Son of the Circus*. In all of his darkly comic work, Irving wrestles with profound issues of faith and doubt — especially doubt — the same way he used to take on opponents as a college wrestler and coach.

Muscled and fit, still weight-training every day, Irving is *GQ*-handsome in his black T-shirt, gray-flannel pants, and shiny black shoes. He writes his long, complex novels, teeming with boisterous characters, the way he answers questions in a small park during a visit to Vancouver from his summer home on one of Georgian Bay's Thirty Thousand Islands. Brooking no interruption, he slowly maneuvers toward each subject, weighing it and toying with it, before whipping it to the mat.

As a youth in New Hampshire, Irving had an on-again, off-again faith. "My parents did what a lot of parents do. They required all of us children to go to church as long as we were children. And then they sent us to schools where we were required to go to church. And then, as soon as we were grown up and out of their care, they stopped going. I don't think they've been to church since, except for weddings or funerals. But it had a bigger effect on me than I think it did on them." His fascination with religion took off when his parents sent him to Exeter Academy boarding school, where chapel was mandatory. There he met the noted Presbyterian theologian and novelist Frederick Buechner. Because he wanted to be a writer, Irving took Buechner's courses at Exeter. Like Irving, Buechner is noted for his profoundly earthy ways of interpreting religion.

"I have had the experience of being moved in church, by the whole feeling of church. I have also had the feeling, as anyone who has gone to church has, of being sincerely put off by what I heard in church. It was the Episcopal Church, which in Canada is the Anglican Church. It is of course beautifully made fun of in Robertson Davies' novel

The Cunning Man, as being somehow more about good behavior and good upbringing and proper diction than it is about any genuine sort of charity." He laughs hard. "And I think it's a very deserved reputation. I would say I was schooled in a religion of snobbery."

According to Irving, the Episcopal Church, which is part of the worldwide Anglican communion, prided itself on not being nearly so offensive as the Catholic Church, nor as outrageously sentimental as the Baptists. "But I mean every religion has little hooks into its counterparts. That's part of the fun of it, isn't it?" Sitting on the park bench, his voice growing more expressive, more rhythmic, staring out at the mansions surrounding this park in Shaughnessy, Vancouver's richest neighborhood, where he gratefully agreed to meet because his hotel room wasn't ready, Irving is warming to his subject.

Perhaps it's a weakness of liberal Christianity that sometimes it has trouble "sticking." Today, Irving, a father of three who travels between residences in Virginia and Canada, considers himself a "holiday churchgoer." In that way he resembles Dr. Daruwalla, the central character in *A Son of the Circus*, an Indian Parsi who immigrated to Toronto and converted to what ends up being a shallow, wavering Anglicanism. Irving sometimes goes to church, mainly at Easter and Christmas, because he likes the music.

"Now, if you push me to the wall, I'd say I'm not a believer. But it depends on the day you ask." He keels over in laughter, pushing his strong hands through solid waves of gray-black hair.

"I'm not being glib. I'm not being funny. I mean, isn't that, to some degree, what agnosticism means? It doesn't seem to me that doubt is the opposite of faith. Doubt is an integral part of faith. I'm not comfortable calling myself a believer, a Christian. But if somebody says, 'Are you an atheist?' I'd back down from that question too. I'd say, 'Listen, I've done a little too much reading and studying about religions in general to ever subscribe to such a simplistic view.'" His voice is professorial and a touch upper-crust. You can almost see the semi-colons as he speaks.

Irving despises it when atheists scoff at people who have faith. "I find religious proselytizers, who insist that we all believe as they do, no more objectionable than atheists who are equally simplistic in wanting the world to agree with them. I find that wanting the world to agree with you is a kind of tyranny."

Irving is a big admirer of Robertson Davies. A year before his death in December 1995, Davies made it clear in a conversation with me that he is more explicitly religious than Irving; yet the two shared Anglicanism and a mutual attraction to both skepticism and faith. Both despised fanatics, a theme that Irving explored in *The World According to Garp*. In *The Manticore*, Davies has a psychologist tell the obsessive Canadian lawyer David Staunton, "You are a fanatic. Don't you know what fanaticism is? It is over-compensation for doubt."

Yet Irving thinks he knows why some literary critics grow skittish with the theological discussions in his novels. When Irving was growing up, religious leaders were a voice for tolerance and understanding. With the help of people such as Buechner, Irving associated Christians with a kind of intellectual liberalism. "This comes, you see, from the Sixties. In the Vietnam period, the church leaders did all they could to heal the enormous divisiveness in the country, to give comfort to soldiers, to give comfort to war resisters — to recognize that was a time that was tearing the country apart and they needed to speak with a voice of tolerance. Martin Luther King came from a similar sort of feeling."

But now he feels that the mood has changed, that the voices of tolerant Christian leaders are drowned out by louder Christians who demonize their opponents. "The contamination of politics by right-wing religious groups in the States and in Canada is one of the things that has given real religion, and truly religious people, a bad name. If you say you're a churchgoer nowadays, what is called to mind are those raving right-to-lifers outside abortion clinics and people wanting to ban books and censor this or that — you know, the kind of uneducated Christian right. A great deal of the book-critic hostility toward *A Prayer for Owen Meany* is, I think, out of the knee-jerk, anti-Christian atheist position, which says, 'God damn it, this is a book about a guy who thinks he's seen a religious miracle, and he tells you in the first sentence he believes in God, therefore John Irving must believe in God too, and therefore he must be an idiot.'"

His speech is picking up vibrancy and emphasis. "It's a very narrow and shortsighted view. But I think it is an understandable reaction to how much we've seen and heard from the religious right. And frankly, I would include the political activities of the Catholic Church in my description of the religious right. Politically, they've sort of allied themselves to that unthinking rabble."

Despite Irving's disappointment with Pope John Paul II, in *A Son of the Circus*, a Jesuit scholastic, a holy fool determined to make Bombay a better place, comes off sympathetically. So does the poor-of-faith Dr. Daruwalla. Yet Irving pokes mischievous fun at both these key characters, as he did at the eccentric Christlike figure in *A Prayer for Owen Meany*, a book which held out Christian faith not as dogma, but as a possibility. Irving delights in making mischief, in upsetting preconceptions, in surprising.

Irving's religious direction isn't as clear in *A Son of the Circus*, where both the Jesuit and Dr. Daruwalla try to help the poor and crippled in a confusing, pluralistic world. The book is laden with ambiguous sexuality, ambiguous identity, and ambiguous religion. Yet the basic decency of Dr. Daruwalla is clear, and Irving shares this semi-spiritual humanism with his character. "Contrary to what many fundamentalist religions would tell us, I don't think the humanist position should be confined to atheists. I think humanism means a belief in the possibility of the goodness of the human being. We are educable; we can be civilized."

Many North Americans who study Eastern mysticism are swept away simply because it is different and exotic. Not so the philosophically sophisticated Irving. He's not about to become a Hindu. But as he researched *A Son of the Circus* in India, his interest in religion did revive again, he says, revealing perhaps that faith and doubt are indeed two sides of the same coin.

Irving pulls out a talisman on a necklace from underneath his shirt. He seems to think twice about whether or not to show it. "Do you think it's a St. Christopher's medal?" he asks playfully. He leans over and reveals a small silver elephant-headed figure with human hands and feet.

"That's Ganesh. Ganesh is the elephant God. He's a very kindly and charitable fellow. He's the one who looks after you," he says. "The man at the circus in Bombay who trained the acrobats gave me this because they were shocked at how much I traveled. He said the acrobats wore them so they wouldn't fall. It's the St. Christopher's idea. If you believe in lucky charms, well, it means your spiritual brain isn't quite dead, right?"

Paul Verhoeven

JOHN LUCAS

*"I don't want to believe if it's not true.
I want evidence!"*

As the tears rolled down his cheeks and new-found Pentecostal friends told him he'd been born again in Jesus Christ, Paul Verhoeven, at age twenty-six, still asked himself: Is this religious salvation or merely a psychological experience? "Even when I was emotionally moved, shaking and on the floor, and everyone around me was speaking in tongues, I felt fooled," says Verhoeven, the director of the Academy Award–nominated foreign-language film *Turkish Delight*, as well as the U.S.-produced thriller *Fatal Instinct* and science-fiction block-busters *RoboCop* and *Total Recall.*

Raised by liberal Christian parents in Holland but never forced to make a commitment to the church, Verhoeven came upon charismatic Christianity after leaving the Dutch navy. He was in turmoil, facing an uncertain future. His short-lived conversion was "extremely explosive." Half of him believed the experience was God taking over his life; the other half that it was just a reconnection with subconscious childhood feelings. "It was like looking at life as a child."

Though he doesn't attend church now, Verhoeven, in his late fifties, is still fascinated, even inspired, by Jesus. He flew to this snow-smothered city of Edmonton from Los Angeles for a conference of a controversial group of New Testament scholars called the Jesus Seminar. He is researching a movie he hopes to direct that will capture the real, historical Jesus, rather than the one he believes mythologized by early Christians. "It will be important to be honest in this Jesus film. I feel it's nonsense to do another movie on the mythic Jesus. I want to know what's true. It's part of the quest for my own belief," he says in his Dutch accent. He and his family moved to the United States in the mid-1980s.

We meet in a University of Alberta seminar room during a break in the proceedings of the Jesus Seminar. His eyes wide and assailable, Verhoeven is laid-back and charming, with a touch of youthful vulnerability. The man who has become one of the world's most provocative and commercially successful film directors, however, claims to carry a stubborn skepticism everywhere.

The Jesus Seminar, founded by Bible specialist Robert Funk, consists of about seventy-five liberal-to-moderate Bible scholars, both professors and Ph.D.s, from some of the world's most respected universities and seminaries — including Burton Mack of Claremont

Graduate School in California, author of *The Lost Gospel*, and Dominique Crossan of DePaul University in Chicago, author of *Jesus: A Revolutionary Biography*. The Seminar scholars meet in different parts of Europe and North America twice a year.

After almost a decade of research, the scholars have concluded that Jesus likely uttered fewer than half of the sayings attributed to him in the New Testament.

Verhoeven first showed up unannounced at a Jesus Seminar conference in California in the late 1980s, where he sat at the back of the room full of scholars and followed their arguments while reading his own biblical texts in the original Greek, which he'd learned to read in school in Holland. He is enthusiastically grateful for the Jesus Seminar's contentious scholarship, which has been published in books such as *The Five Gospels*.

"I always find myself interested in the sources of the sources of the sources," he says. While obtaining a Ph.D. in physics and mathematics, Verhoeven learned that "nothing is clean, nothing is provable." He is like a modern Doubting Thomas — the disciple who had to poke his finger in Jesus' bloody wound before believing he was the son of God returned. Verhoeven does not have the luxury of being face-to-face with Jesus. Yet his burning analytical mind is pushing him to recreate, as exactly and truthfully as possible, the life and times of the historical Jesus.

Verhoeven explains that the Dutch psyche tends toward hardheadedness. "There is a respect for reality." He points to the work of the great seventeenth-century Dutch realist painters such as Rembrandt, who were so frank they included in their work such things as people urinating against buildings. "There's very few people who would put that in a painting." When he was making the futuristic *Total Recall*, starring Arnold Schwarzenneger and Sharon Stone,

Verhoeven's drive for authenticity led him to read scientific journals about Mars to find out such things as whether the atmosphere would appear pink or blue. He pored over history books when working on *Soldier of Orange*, a realistic portrayal of the Dutch resistance during the Nazi occupation of Holland, which he endured as a child. "That's the way I operate in a lot of cases. For me it's always very important to feel secure about what's real."

Since none of the authors of the gospels of Matthew, Mark, Luke, and John knew Jesus personally, Verhoeven says the sources for their accounts were stories passed on orally around tables and fires. At the Jesus Seminar, the gathered scholars are asked to drop different colored beads into a box to show whether they think a New Testament passage about Jesus is authentic (red bead), possibly authentic (pink bead), a probable fabrication of gospel writers (gray bead), or definitely not authentic (black bead). Verhoeven says the stripped-down portrait of the historical Jesus that remains after this sorting shows a man who loosely resembles the popular image of Gandhi.

"Jesus was not a big deal to most people at the time. Pilate didn't even want to bother with him. He saw Jesus as a nobody. He was like a Dutch resistance fighter during the Second World War. He was just someone that Pilate thought should be dead." In a paper Verhoeven delivered to the Jesus Seminar, he calls Jesus "a social rebel who sought a non-military revival of Israel . . . a Jewish peasant at odds with his mother and brothers . . . who wandered the country and told people of his unique vision of God, saying God's kingdom already existed on earth . . . who taught followers to heal the sick in God's name . . . who made enemies of the powerful by siding with outcasts . . . who broke the taboo against befriending women but had more important things on his mind than sex . . . who challenged Jewish religious laws and an unjust tax-collection system . . . and was crucified, almost nonchalantly, by the occupying Roman military."

Verhoeven believes Jesus was completely human. "But I don't think we should be arrogant enough to say he was also not God. It's not impossible. Even in physics, there's not much we can really be sure about. Materialism is only one way of looking at things." Nevertheless, if he had to vote on whether he believed Jesus was divine, he'd probably cast a gray bead (for probably not), perhaps a pink (for possibly). The same goes for the questions of whether God exists. "For me, it would be much nicer to believe in God. But I don't know if God exists. I don't know what God is," he says, his voice becoming high and excited. "And so I cannot make up my mind. I will say very clearly that there is not enough evidence to say that the existence of God is impossible."

He thinks Christ for most people functions as a Jungian archetype, a mythic symbol of the collective human unconscious, for those who hope to survive death. "The real Jesus is hidden behind the Jungian archetype. The Jesus archetype says our dying is not the ultimate situation. There is a way to escape. Christian belief suggests there is a possibility beyond death. That is a reassuring possibility for me," he says. "My first girlfriend, the girl that I was probably in love with when I was fifteen, she still essentially believes that. She is Catholic and living in London and I think her belief provides a lot of comfort and strength for her. So why wouldn't you believe it if it's true? It would be silly not to! It's the best thing that could happen. But I don't want to believe it if it's not true."

Verhoeven's appetite for honesty extends beyond religion, to his personal life. He believes it's right, for example, for a spouse to tell the other about an affair. "It can do a lot of damage, but you don't want the other partner to be living in a false world. You have to be prepared to lose the people you address." His marriage to Martina, who is in her early fifties, survived such a confession of his.

Verhoeven has a tortured imagination that continually raises the specter of his own death and a possibly demonic otherworld. He would like to believe in a pleasant afterlife. "I think what I've been doing since I was eighteen is trying to believe in some possibility of life after death. But, being so dialectic about it, I don't want to believe if it's not true. I want evidence!" he says, with a pained smile.

Because Verhoeven fears death, he'd also like to believe in some sort of heaven, not a hell. "I've had, in my own life, terrible dreams about my own death. The essence of the dream is a feeling of hell. It is complete isolation of the soul. Complete aloneness." Nevertheless, he can't, intellectually, take the final step and accept that Jesus was resurrected and the rest of humanity will rise up to heaven. And although Verhoeven has worked intensely with the scholars of the Jesus Seminar, many of whom are liberal Christians, he cannot accept the view that faith relies not on the factual accuracy of the Bible but on "trust" in a mysterious God who cannot be fully captured by any book or doctrine. "I just don't want to cheat," Verhoeven says, obviously frustrated with his own rationality.

Despite his push for objectivity (which many philosophers say is impossible, because everyone sees the world from a particular point of view), after stripping Jesus of what he considers mythological embellishments, Verhoeven finds "there's still mystery there." He hopes his film about the historical Jesus, which is a long-term project that he doesn't know when he will make, will encourage more people to investigate Jesus. He plans to portray a Jesus that will offer people "support."

Asked what he values most, he says "My work and my children are the most important to me." Work keeps him "sane." It gives pleasure and contact with people, and keeps him so busy that he can forget his darker musings. As for his children, he says, "If I was asked to give my life for somebody I would hesitate in 99 percent of the cases because of my heavy doubts of conservation of life after death. In dying, you lose everything. Even if the soul survives, it doesn't guarantee it will go to something that is good. In the Greek way of thinking, the soul went to the shadow world. The Greek hero Achilles said it is better to be the lowest servant on earth than to be the king of the underworld." But Verhoeven would willingly die for his two children.

Could it actually be love, spiritual love, that would make him sacrifice himself despite his fear of death? "Maybe," he says. Then he smiles and returns reluctantly to his skeptical, materialistic view of reality: "Love for children is partly just instinct."

Laurence Gough

BILL KEAY

"I don't want to come across like a saint here — because I'm not,
I can be a jerk — but I think the best thing you can do is forgive.
The most selfish thing you can do is forgive."

As I walk past the giant evergreen hedge up to the Tudor-style house in Kerrisdale, one of Vancouver's tonier neighborhoods near the forested University of British Columbia campus, my mind races. What am I getting into? I am here to interview one of the most successful crime writers in North America about, of all things, morality and spirituality.

Laurence Gough's work is tough and bleak. Britain's *Mail on Sunday* has called Gough's books about detectives Jack Willows and

Claire Parker "bitter, bloody, and brilliantly compulsive." The *Washington Post* has said Gough's writing is as "tight as a trigger." One of the latest in his seven-book crime series, the darkly humorous *Killers*, swirls around the death of a creepy biologist, whose body is found in the killer whale pool at the Vancouver Public Aquarium.

When I step up on Gough's porch, I'm therefore half-prepared to meet a cynical Mr. Cool, wearing shades even though it's January.

I am surprised when Gough answers the door a split second after I ring. It seems kind of polite.

"Nice joint," I say, trying to act casual. It's a dumb comment, but it's true: his home is casual, gabled, and big. He can afford big; Gough has sold about a million books, which have been translated into thirteen languages. His crime novels are a hit in Britain and Europe, and so is his thriller, *Sandstorm*. In Japan, publishers print 50,000 paperback copies of each novel. Gough walks me in to his quiet, slightly disheveled living room. He is lean and tight as a black belt, but his face is softer than the hard-edged photos of him that appear on his book jackets. Truth to tell, he looks damned fine for a guy in his fifties.

I open by saying he's been compared to the famous American crime writer Elmore Leonard. Leonard, despite writing about the seediest of the seedy, is a devout Catholic.

That's the ironic thing about mysteries, Gough suggests. Even though they're written as entertainment, "crime novels are all about morality: crime and punishment. That's what's responsible for a lot of their appeal."

With such insights, it soon becomes obvious that Gough is a reflective guy. He's also willing to reveal some knocks in his early days. He is hardly an orthodox believer. When growing up in Greater Vancouver, his mother, an Anglican, sometimes took him to church. There was a rifle-shooting range in one Burnaby church basement. He enjoyed shooting, but it wasn't exactly the Sermon on the Mount.

He was "a typical caustic young guy." He didn't know his biological father well, and didn't get along with his stepfather, who moved in when Laurence was about four. As a boy, he was arrested for shoplifting enough ballpoint pens to fill his jacket. Later, he slung garbage, then worked in a bookstore. Around his early thirties, he began writing radio dramas for the CBC.

He became a househusband to raise his teenage boys, Morgan and Dashiell (who was *not* named after the great mystery writer, Dashiell Hammett). "I'm a pretty masculine person. I can be insensitive. But I think, in other ways, I was the new man before the new man was in vogue," he says. "I've been a househusband all my married life. I think it made me pretty aware of the feminine side of life."

Gough took up mystery writing after yet another budget cut at the CBC in 1984. He chose to have both a male and a female detective at the center of his books because he wanted to write about a strong woman. "Claire Parker is just as strong as Jack Willows in my books. But she's also more in control of herself. She has that advantage over Willows. I'm really comfortable with it."

His wife, part-time lawyer Jan Rose, is also a strong woman, he acknowledges. Just then his big, laid-back dog walks in, hairy and shedding — good company for a writer. He's alone in the house most weekdays, while his wife works and children attend school.

From his early books, *Death on a #8 Hook* and *Serious Crimes,* to 1996's *Heartbreaker,* the relationship between Jack Willows and Claire Parker has evolved in a friendly, mature way. Gough avoids tiresome gender wars, and mainly lets these two world-weary characters enjoy each other's company. He's not claiming his books are high art. But they do have threads of meaning and a liberating humor, which keeps Gough feeling he's writing something a little redemptive, not just mayhem. In his later books, he believes, the characters have become better at self-discovery.

The body count is also steadily going down in Gough's crime novels. In his first, *The Goldfish Bowl*, nine people wind up dead as tuna bait. Three die in *Killers*. His next crime book will have fewer deaths. "In my first book, when the characters ran into a brick wall, the easiest way out was to kill people. But I thought if I could get away with less violence, I'd do that. As you become more aware of your craft, you develop the skills that allow you to do that."

He also considers pontificating to be bad writing. "I wouldn't want to be a seller of morality. I don't want to preach. I think, inevitably, what's more important is how we express our beliefs in our day-to-day lives." When he's out walking with his kids, for example, he'll give to beggars and tell the kids about good and bad luck in life. "My mother taught us that things come back to you. I think when you give out, you receive."

A few social issues are beginning to appear in his books, however. *Killers*, for example, criticizes putting whales in captivity. "I don't think I have any friends at the aquarium," he says. On the other hand, the book also includes a couple of dangerously fundamentalist environmentalists.

Even though Gough's plots invariably begin with grisly murders, the underlying theme of his crime series, he insists, is love — people who need love and don't get it, people who don't trust anybody, people who struggle to make a life together, and people who throw themselves into love and come out whole.

A recent pivotal event made him examine love and mortality in his own life. His stepfather died; Gough was the only one in the nursing home room with him.

"At the moment of his death, there was actually a very strong physical change. There was a real sense of evacuation in my father's body.

It wasn't a shiny white light or anything. But there was a real sense of rustling in the air — a sense he had risen up out of himself, of something leaving him when he died. And not just life itself. But something far more powerful than that."

The death occurred at 2 a.m. "It was a wonderful experience. I wasn't frightened by it. But I was certainly moved by it, astounded by it, because I had not anticipated anything like it."

From that moment on, Gough took much more seriously the possibility of life after death. "I don't see clouds or harps, or anything like that, but I think if there is any life after death, it would possibly be a kind of blending of spirits — maybe some resultant force that comes out of life and death. Obviously it's nothing but speculation. But what happened when my father died was so vivid and so powerful and so real, yet so strange, that I knew when I was leaving the home that I would start to turn on myself and I would start not to trust myself and what I'd seen. I was determined not to do that. When I talked to people about what happened, there was often some skepticism. But the whole experience has made me feel stronger about the probability of faith. I feel a lot more religious now."

To emphasize his inner conversion, he walks to his computer and calls up a letter he has just sent to his New York agent outlining his next non-crime book, an adventure romance. He reads aloud: "What I'm trying to write about is the leathery toughness of the human spirit, about man's inhumanity to man, the importance of love, the need to atone for one's sins, and the absolute necessity to forgive those who have trespassed against you."

Those words, which Gough can hardly believe he wrote, reflect some of the tension he tried to resolve with his workaholic stepfather before he died. Gough often felt his stepfather treated his biological children better than him. However, after his stepfather became sick,

Gough made a genuine effort to get to know him and put his resentment behind him.

"I think my stepfather had a lot of unfinished business. And I had a lot of negative feelings about it. It took me a long time to realize he was treating his own children the same way he was treating me, that I was not singled out for neglect. I don't want to come across like a saint here — because I'm not, I can be a jerk — but I think the best thing you can do is forgive. The most selfish thing you can do is forgive. I think freedom's found through forgiveness." His voice is tender.

"I think we all disappoint ourselves, and you learn from that. I remember when I was younger holding such firm feelings about things. I still have plenty of convictions, but I'm a lot less inclined to point the finger now. We are all rehatched every day. The experience we had the previous day affects how we are today. With parenting, every day is a wonderful opportunity to fall flat on your face."

When it comes time to say goodbye, Gough lingers on his porch. In the afternoon sun, he seems eager to continue our discussion. Most of his close friends, he says, are uncomfortable talking about God and such. "I'm thinking about going to the United Church down the road. But part of the problem is the kids. When we talk about religion around the table, they're very cynical about it, and I don't think they picked it up from me."

Keeping an eye out for the boys coming home from school, his voice is woundable as he says, "I have my religious moments, usually when I come across little set pieces walking in the park around UBC. That's where I feel closest to the idea that something put all this together. But I think I've been undecided all my life."

Evelyn Lau

IAN LINDSAY

"I take issue with poets who say some days it just descends from the clouds in inspiration. I really dislike the idea that you're just being a conduit for a larger force that is doing all the work for you. I mean it is such hard work."

Evelyn Lau — acclaimed writer, ex-prostitute, former drug addict — starts out claiming she's an atheist. She does not now, nor has she ever, believed in life after death, in revering ancestors, or in being good. And she's not so sure about love, either. Yet, in her mid-twenties, she is full of youthful contradictions on all counts.

Almost as an afterthought, she tosses out this: "Ah. But I have devised, ever since I was about eight years old, my own personal god.

And he looked after nobody else but me." She gives an embarrassed, disarming laugh. It sneaks out often during our long talk at the upscale Star Anise restaurant in Vancouver, where she suggested we have lunch, and where she reveals an instinctive understanding of the spiritual idea that confession is good for the soul.

"I was a very selfish little kid. And he was my writing god. I would talk to him every night. And I would pray to him as though I was praying to any other god," she says brightly, picking up a glass of white wine with her freckled hand. Alcohol is the only drug she uses now.

"His role in my life was to look after my writing. He was going to make sure I was going to be a writer, a good writer, and achieve recognition. In exchange, I would never ask him for anything else. If my health was bad, if bad things happened to me, I could not ask him for help because he did not look after those areas of my life. And the silly thing is, when something good happens to me with my writing, like when I was nominated for the Governor General's Award, or I've signed a new book contract, I still pause for a moment in my life and thank him."

She must be talking a lot to him. Lau's best-selling autobiography, *Runaway: Diary of a Street Kid*, was turned into a CBC movie of the same name. She has written two books of award-winning poetry, as well as *Fresh Girls*, a collection of disturbing, erotic short stories that has been translated into five languages. Clarissa Pinkola Estes, author of *Women Who Run with the Wolves*, has called *Fresh Girls* "stark, compelling, and poignant." W. P. Kinsella is one of Lau's biggest fans and supporters.

Lau is also starting to like herself more. Her dead-eyed, painted-doll appearance of only a few years ago has been replaced with a softer, Greenwich-Village look: red lipstick, casually styled hair, baggy black sweater and black pants.

She is a budding literary iconoclast who acknowledges, with fetching honesty, that she is still sorting out her beliefs. Lau would be the first to declare that her personal god is not the God of higher universal purpose discussed in better churches, synagogues, and temples. But her god may be the kind many actually cling to in the privacy of their hearts: a made-to-order guardian angel.

At age thirteen, Lau, wearing gawky glasses and a humble smile, met Pope John Paul II. She was not Catholic. In fact, she had internalized her Asian immigrant parents' mockery of all things religious, from Judaism to Christianity to Buddhism to Chinese ancestor worship. She just wanted to be a writer, a recognized writer. So she entered a *Vancouver Sun* essay contest that asked: What would you like to tell the Pope? Being a passionate girl, she wrote about the horror of nuclear war.

She thereby won the chance to meet the Pope during his 1984 Vancouver visit. "This will sound terrible, but I had no interest in meeting the Pope. Why would I want to meet the Pope?" Nevertheless, because she wanted to be a journalist, and she thought the profession unfairly maligned, she seized her moment in the receiving line to ask the Pope to bless journalists. John Paul asked her to repeat herself. She couldn't understand his murmured answer, but John Paul did bless a rosary and give it to her.

Back then Lau was sweet and demure on the outside, but rebellion exploded within her. She hated her parents, who forbade her writing and expected her to be a doctor. Within two years of meeting the Pope, Lau had run away from her east Vancouver home. She was taking LSD and heroin, turning tricks in cars and apartments, trying to commit suicide, being confined to psychiatric wards, and living in group homes.

Remarkably, after all that self-destructive turmoil, the rosary still hangs on the bedroom wall of her rented apartment. If nothing else, she says, it reminds her of being published. "It's just there. I just look at it and I smile. I think it's funny that I have kept it — that it's moved through everything I've done."

It is difficult for others to imagine, she says, how obsessed she is with being a writer. Since the age of six, using her talent to the full, and being recognized for it, has been her life's purpose. Though self-disgust slashes through her life and art ("I was trash. I was a slut. I want to disown this body now, cast it forever to the winds. It is too gross to be mine," she writes in *Runaway*), she clings to writing as the best part of her. "It was the one thing about me that was pure."

As a child, she thought her writing would do good by giving pleasure. When she was on the streets, she wanted to "show people a part of life that is not really seen, generate some compassion for those people on the edge who would normally be made fun of. I wanted to show the humanness and isolation of it all." Now her aim in writing is to illuminate language and articulate the experience and the feelings of others. "It's probably the closest to selfless I ever come."

Lau has paradoxical feelings about writing. While she made a pact for success with a personal writing god, she rejects the notion put forth by some writers and artists who credit their creativity in part to a kind of divine force field that helps draw them out. "I take issue with poets in particular who say some days it just descends from the clouds in inspiration," she says. "I really dislike the idea that you're just being a conduit for a larger force that is doing all the work for you. I mean it is such hard work."

When Lau was a child, she put such faith in the near-mystical power of writing that she even thought it would protect her from death. Later, as a prostitute, she had to confront a great deal more. She exposes herself to violent movies to calm her fear of death. She still wonders if her writing is a kind of talisman protecting her — she hopes it will give her at least literary immortality. "Intellectually, I don't believe in living forever or in an afterlife. But I'd love to be proved wrong. In some sly little part of my brain, I think maybe I'm exempt."

It's not in Lau's nature to hide anything, from kinky sex to character flaws. Her worldview is evolving (she dropped out of school in grade ten) as she devours the work of the best fiction writers, including her hero, John Updike, and boldly explores the breadth and depth of experience. Just as she too quickly claimed to being an atheist who doesn't accept an afterlife, however, she too swiftly dismisses the idea that she cares about being good.

Her ethical struggling is revealed when she hauls out a large envelope that shows how her hooker past has just caught up with her again. A man has sent a cryptic letter asking her, since she must have several "regulars," to set aside fifteen minutes to "talk" with him and autograph her book. A $100 bill is attached. What was the guy after? Should she meet him? She asks for advice about the right thing to do. Not long ago, she says she would have kept the $100. I suggest sending the money back with no comment. She goes for that.

Money has always been a source of conflict for Lau. As a teen, she wrote about millions of dollars being wasted on Vancouver's Expo '86. For a short time she served as a far-left activist. Now she finds it painful to pay taxes on her book royalties. She's currently absorbed in capitalism, and has bought her first apartment, which she deeply wishes could have been a Shaughnessy mansion. She ended up writing a personal essay about it.

She admits, "some of my friends say, 'We would have liked you better back when you cared about things. Now you just care about real estate.'" She attributes her concern for money to the uncertainty of being homeless. To her credit, she recognizes that, as some friends have told her, she'll probably never send in enough taxes to pay back the government for the shelter, food, and psychotherapy she received while she worked the streets.

She is still sifting through the morality of the sex trade. During her years as a prostitute, she says, she took money to perform virtually every sex act imaginable.

How did she feel about it? The short answer is "ashamed."

"Sometimes I pretended I was in control," she explains, "but in reality she felt she had no choice. She was addicted to prostitution, to the money, and to the strange appreciation she felt for sexually satisfying someone — an appreciation she had never felt from her parents.

"The funny thing now is I am actually quite moral about sex. It raises my eyebrows when friends sleep with a person on the first date. Even as a prostitute, I frowned on promiscuity. I would have thought it was promiscuous to sleep with someone just because I liked them."

She has often imagined it would be nice to be the wife instead of the hooker, perhaps even one who is being cheated on. But she has had virtually no experience of relationships, and doesn't know if she ever will. What does it take to love someone? "I can be vulnerable with my work. I can be vulnerable like this, in a conversation with you. But I can't imagine being vulnerable with a partner. I mean, boy, all my defences would come out. That's the frustrating thing."

Her independence gives her an unusual perspective, she says with a wry smile, from which to write about infidelity, the subject of her latest novel, *Other Women*.

Although Lau welcomes the wine with lunch, it is the dessert she most enjoys. Offering to share, she excitedly dives into blueberry-and-pineapple sherbet. She is hypoglycemic, and later blames the sugar for making her too confessional.

She never talks to her personal god when she's in despair, she says. That's not his department. "The only time I talk to him is when something I'm proud about has happened. I thank him. But I must say, I must say, there was one time in my life when I tried to take back that deal I made."

She hesitates for more than a minute, saying "umm" five times. She has bared her tortured soul and body for all the world, but this is obviously something even harder. Finally she blurts out, "I was for the first and only time in my life in love. And I said to him, 'If I could have this, you could go away.'"

A scratch etches her voice. If she had said the words more slowly, she probably would have cried. She is once again a fragile girl in a street-smart woman, yearning for love, not really believing she deserves it.

"But it didn't happen." She laughs. "So. I'm back where I started."

Maybe she could have both, I suggest: writing and love.

She dismisses the possibility. The droning old message of unworthiness pounds.

"That would be an embarrassment of riches, wouldn't it?"

Would it?

She hesitates. "I wonder."

Wade Davis

BRIAN KENT

"To witness sane and in every regard respectable individuals experiencing direct rapport with the divine fills one with either fear, which finds its natural outlet in disbelief, or envy."

The man on the telephone from Louisiana told the TV host he'd pay $1,000 if Wade Davis would come down and remove the curse on him. It typified the calls that flooded in when Davis appeared on *Good Morning America* to answer questions about his exploits among the Voodoo followers of Haiti, where Davis had ventured to research zombies — people who had been drugged, buried alive, and resurrected from the grave.

The Harvard-trained Canadian ethnobotanist seized the public's imagination with his best-selling book about zombies, *The Serpent and the Rainbow*, which inspired a high-grossing Hollywood movie of the same name. Davis has been dubbed a "real-life Indiana Jones." *Newsweek* called his book a "swashbuckling scientific adventure story."

The loquacious Davis is fascinated with what he calls the thin veil between this world and what may be the spirit world. Unlike some agnostics, who can't believe in divinity because they have never seen a miracle or had a paranormal experience, Davis has seen it all. But he refuses to start worshipping something he doesn't fully understand.

While his two young children play in his West Vancouver home, we walk out among the trees in his backyard to the converted garage that serves as his office. He is tall, thin, energetic, and fresh-looking for a man in his early forties.

He views the call from the man who believed he was cursed as an indication of how thirsty North Americans are for supernatural experience. "It also reveals how gullible people can be." He points out that someone with academic credentials exploring alternative realities, like his pal and occasional co-author Dr. Andrew Weil, could haul in a lot of money on the New Age circuit. But Davis is on a more subtle, uncertain, and wise spiritual expedition. To his mind, too many people entirely give up their critical faculties to have faith. "The closed-minded U.S. religious right is giving Christianity a bad name," he says. "But the New Age movement isn't a lot better. Its motto seems to be: 'If I believe it, then it's true.'"

As an ethnobotanist, i.e., someone who studies the cultural use of plants, Davis harnesses his discerning intellect to serve his passion for nature, the unexplained, and the sacred. In his inspired examinations of Voodoo religion, South American shamanistic healing, and hallucinogenic plants, he does not shirk from using the term "spirits."

Moist and feral, his hillside West Vancouver property conjures up visions of the jungle forest where Davis has pursued his career. His office contains spears, shields, antelope skulls, and feathers in addition to bulging file folders, walls of botanical and anthropological books and essays, and detailed maps of the world's jungles, forests, and deserts. His home is surrounded by walls of luxuriant foliage, which his neighbors tell him block their coveted, property-value-increasing view of the Strait of Georgia. He shrugs.

Years ago, Davis jumped when one of his Harvard professors suggested he travel to Haiti to look for the Voodoo potion that was used to turn people into zombies. But he found more than a secret drug called tetrodotoxin. He found a complex culture that gives many Haitians — not to mention zombies — an astounding day-to-day relationship with what they believe is the divine.

Davis saw people, apparently possessed by spirits, dancing, thrashing, and spinning to the beat of drums. He saw men chew glass and swallow fire without experiencing physical harm. He saw tiny, possessed women grab big men and swing them about like children. His eyes still widen with amazement as he describes these sights.

Haiti was an epiphany for Davis. "For the nonbeliever, there is something profoundly disturbing about spirit possession. Its power is raw, immediate, and undeniably real, devastating in a way to those of us who do not know our gods," he writes in *Whispered Messages of the Wild*.

"To witness sane and in every regard respectable individuals experiencing direct rapport with the divine fills one with either fear, which finds its natural outlet in disbelief, or envy," the passage continues. "To the believer, the dissociation of personality that characterizes possession is the hand of divine grace; to the psychologist it is but a symptom of an 'overwhelming psychic disturbance.'"

Davis is among the envious. He has a low opinion of "the secret society of scientists and psychologists who contemptuously deny any other possibilities." He has not reached a final conclusion, but remains open to the possibility that he is studying phenomena influenced by divinity. As a kind of mystical agnostic, he resembles the eighteenth-century English poet William Wordsworth, who refused to name the spirit he found in nature as anything more than "something" because he was concerned with accuracy of expression. That "something" did not fit any categories Wordsworth knew.

Raised in West Vancouver in the early 1950s, Davis started out with an instinctual faith in God. Although his parents criticized organized religion, Davis as a preteen went virtually every week with a friend to the United Church of Canada. "I remember religiously saying my prayers at night," he says, adding, "I made up most of them." He recalls pushing his window open on freezing nights and "sitting there in my pyjamas and just looking at the stars. I just knew God was there."

By his early teens, however, his spontaneous faith began to disappear. He was turned off by the sterility of the church and a history of church wrongs. He found, like many of his generation, that eventually his "belief in God got transferred to a love of nature."

Davis respected his father, an inward-looking man of few words, quite the opposite of the extroverted, devil-may-care Davis, who says he was "born to be a grandfather sitting around telling lies." Because of his father's aloof, introspective nature, however, Davis spent much of his twenties looking for mentors; his search led him to native elders in Canada's north, Harvard professors, and Latin American shamans.

During Davis's risk-taking days he traveled to Haiti, South America, the Arctic, and almost anywhere else one could name. He got lost in giant swamps, ate carpenter ants to build a rapport with natives, slept with a lot of women, and ingested more than a few hallucinogenic drugs — partly in the name of research.

His philosophy of life amounted to saying "Yes! Yes! Yes!" to any new experience. It is a faithful and mystical attitude of sorts to believe the universe exists for one's enjoyment.

But something larger took a firm hold of Davis's insides in 1985 when his father died. Davis was hanging out in a remote Spanish town when he heard the news. While waiting to catch a flight back to Canada, he spent twelve hours by himself with nothing to do but ponder his place in the cosmos. "I truly felt the presence of God then. I truly felt my father was with me. Right then my life changed." He moved back to Canada, married, and had children. "I felt a tremendous visceral sense that I'm next [to die] and a tremendous sense I had to procreate."

He returned to West Vancouver, buying a house less than ten blocks from where his parents had lived when he was born. Borrowing a concept from Hinduism, he explains that this began the "householder" phase of his life. "I've become more humble," he says, helping others find enjoyment instead of putting all his energy into his own. According to American philosopher John Cobb, such a focus can be the foundation of a profound ethical system. Davis now devotes his time to his family, lecturing, research, and protecting the environment. One of his latest projects is protecting the Cassiar region of northern British Columbia, a thirty-two-million-acre expanse of mountains, rivers, and boreal forest. Some call the area the Serengeti of Canada because of its vast array of wildlife, which includes wolves, caribou, grizzly bears, sheep, and mountain goats.

Just as he envies the all-pervasive spirituality of native Indians and Haitians, Davis envies the tangible spirituality of his children and his wife, Gail, who attends the Christian Science Church in West Vancouver and believes that mystical and physical healing go together. The World Health Organization, Davis says, reports that 80 percent of global medicine is based on this worldview. He has seen women who become fertile after a chicken is sacrificed in front of them. He has seen Voodoo acolytes eat burning embers with impunity. He has seen miraculous recoveries.

He has written: "Many of the ideas that lie at the very heart of shamanistic healing — ideas concerning the spiritual realm, mind-body interactions, and the interplay among humanity, the environment, and the cosmos — are summarily dismissed by Western medicine because they don't fit into its scientific model. Health and illness fall too close to the complicated mysteries that lie at the heart of existence — mysteries of balance, of the mind and the body, of death and the dream of rebirth — for medicine to ever be a hard science."

Despite his openness to such mysteries, Davis feels he is far from the end of his spiritual journey. When he says it would be terrible to die not knowing faith, he reveals a longing to make contact with a more palpable, more powerful, spiritual reality. Perhaps agnosticism is a stage for him, as it was for Sir Francis Bacon, who wrote that we should not begin our spiritual journey with certainty, because it would inevitably end in doubt.

Davis realizes his thoughts on his own journey have gelled a little even during our talk. "It's not great to hold orthodox beliefs in your twenties, when you should pursue adventure," he says, his eyes sparkling impishly. They turn somber when he wisely adds, "Faith should grow gradually as you deal with the pain and joy of existence, the deaths and births. True religious faith has to be honed by the beauty and tragedy of life."

$\mathscr{D}ouglas\ \mathscr{C}oupland$

"I can't imagine life without curiosity."

When Douglas Coupland returns to Vancouver from Europe, he is always depressed. So he immediately heads for the wet evergreen forests and plunging rock walls of Capilano Canyon, near his North Shore home, where he can lose himself in nature. He doesn't exactly "find God" (he considers the phrase a cliché), but he finds something.

"There's a kind of purity there, isn't there? There's this weird sacred thing," he says, drinking beer in Ya Ya's Oyster Bar, a seaside haunt

83

about twenty minutes northwest of Vancouver.

After Europe's mind-assault of history and culture, which "makes the sensitive part of you seize up," Coupland says, he can't wait to get into the forest near his home where he played as a kid. It's a key to who he is.

The land plays a crucial part in many of Coupland's books, especially *Life After God*, in which the narrator, at the end of an agonizing search for meaning outside politics and religion, has an epiphany while naked in a frigid, burbling stream: "My secret is that I need God — that I am sick and can no longer make it alone," the narrator confesses. "I need God to help me give, because I no longer seem to be capable of giving; to help me be kind, as I no longer seem capable of kindness; to help me love, as I seem beyond being able to love."

The passage is especially revealing since Coupland freely admits his characters reflect part of his personality. "It's not like UFOs came down and made up the characters," he says. It's a strange, engaging experience to interview him. The lanky author of *Generation X*, which is often cited as a defining novel of the post-baby-boom generation, *Shampoo Planet*, *Life After God*, and *Microserfs*, which together have sold millions of copies and inspired several internet web sites, may be Canada's most notorious author. He rarely gives interviews, and when he does, he won't allow them to follow any usual course. He says he turns them "upside down, sideways, or backwards."

Ours became a conversation. With his hypersensitivity to the semiotics of his physical surroundings (the "meaning" of his sunglasses, for instance), he often digresses, pauses, skips topics, evades questions, stutters, or allows his sentences to disintegrate repeatedly into "like, you know," as he chases a new thought. It's both frustrating and fun.

In this session, he asks me as many questions as I ask him. It turns out Coupland and I share being raised on the edge of two feral North

Shore wilderness parks. My backyard was Lynn Canyon. Three miles to the west, his playground was Capilano Canyon. He thinks the West Coast, particularly British Columbia, with its vast wilderness, lack of institutional history, and dearth of clear codes to live by, may be giving birth to a new worldview.

"I mean, look out the window," he says. We sit at a small table at the bar window, which looks out at passersby, the black-green waters of Howe Sound, and the giant ferries docking at Horseshoe Bay ferry terminal. He gestures toward the steep mountains diving into the sound. "You can never get tired of this. It's one of the few things in life that's renewable, like hair. It always comes back. I read somewhere that the French only like nature after it's been modified by man. So even their gardens are meant to be viewed from the air. I mean, basically, nature is a bore to the French, which I can't understand."

People on the West Coast, he suggests, might not be able to define the worldview that is emerging out of their region "for another two hundred years or something. But there's something that's going to come out of here, out of this part of the world. I can feel it. I don't know what it is."

When I ask if this is a new "spirituality," he snaps, "No. No. No." He's tired of words like "spirituality" and "religion." He also doesn't like to hear the word "mystic" to describe himself. He hates labels, especially those applied to him.

"The moment you say 'spiritual' you get right off into ashrams and things like that. You don't hear much about the New Age any more, do you?" Astrology, reflexology, and aromatherapy, says Coupland, are as orthodox as Catholicism. "They all say they aren't, but they are." His voice softens, as if he's not enjoying criticizing.

When I tell him British Columbia has one of the highest proportions in North America of residents who have no religion whatsoever, he is not surprised. About 30 percent of British Columbians tell census takers they have no religious affiliation, compared to averages of about 10 percent nationwide in both Canada and the United States. He believes British Columbia is one of the toughest places in the world to figure out who you are. "You're from the West Coast, so you know what it's like. Here you're just catapulted out into the universe and you're expected to find something with no foundation, no framework, no anything."

Although he was born on a Canadian NATO base in Germany in 1961, Coupland has spent much of his life in Greater Vancouver. He grew up with three brothers, his doctor father, and his mother, a homemaker with a bachelor's degree in comparative religion from Queen's University in Kingston, Ontario, "who is now Ms. Secular." He thinks he had a pleasant childhood, although he can't remember much of it, which is fine with him. "There's this maxim that goes, 'You shouldn't have a childhood that's too good or too bad, because you'll spend your life either trying to recapture it or denying it.'"

Coupland has never gone to church, except for weddings, even though three great-grandfathers were Presbyterian ministers. Both his parents, he says, "tried to eradicate the religious bugbears of their past. I got the trickle-down. I see all these [religious] slots that people have built, but mine are completely empty." Other than old friends from his youth, he finds himself clicking the most these days with struggling Catholics or Jews.

Six months before he could be pinned down to a time for this interview, he agreed readily over the phone in principle to a talk about what I would call "spiritual" issues, although he wouldn't utter the word. He told me he considers it crucial to be thinking about such things — in fact, he wished it were part of everyday dinner conversations and parties. "There's nothing more I'd like to see than Christianity becoming relevant," he told me over his cordless phone; I could hear him crashing around in his kitchen. More than 75 percent of North Americans, I said, tell pollsters they believe Jesus is divine. "But how much of that is responsible for the Edmonton Mall and Edgemont Village? That's my world. I can't pretend ancient Mesopotamia is my world. People ask me why I write about the middle class. It's because I'm fucking middle class. You write about what you know."

When, months later, we meet in this jangling bar, he returns to the relevance of religious belief. Despite the earnest efforts of North Shore churches to integrate with the mountain environment by designing their buildings like A-frame lodges, they still seem out of place to Coupland. He feels orthodox religious packages are "beside the point." Even people who claim they believe in the divinity of Jesus (or follow the teachings of Buddha, about which he admits to knowing nothing) are probably shaped less by their religion, he says, than by their physical surroundings.

"No one is actually looking at the world around them, you know," he says, picking up the glass salt-and-pepper shakers, then pointing at my black-and-purple canvas carrying bag. The bag's label is from the Mountain Equipment Co-op, a giant Canadian outdoor recreation supply company based in Vancouver. When high-style urbanites visit Coupland from New York City, he says, they always rush to Mountain Equipment Co-op to buy turquoise anoraks and purple fleece jackets. "Like, Mountain Equipment Co-op is a fact of life to us. But everything we take for granted here is exotic to virtually everyone else on the planet. The lifestyle of the employees at Mountain Equipment is as crystalline and pure as crack. And you can join. It's weird. We're lost. But we have this unbelievable set of new symbols and meanings around us. And all we have to do is open our eyes and look a bit harder and figure out how they relate and what the new mythologies are.

"People yearn for meaning," he says, "and they are not finding it in fiction. Self-help books are having to fill some sort of stopgap need, but they're not doing a great job." Today's fiction doesn't explore the real visceral things of life, he says, taking in the table top and a blonde couple outside on the sidewalk. "How do you construct a — help me with this word here — a cosmology in a world of Lucite menu holders and Sony tape recorders and German tourists? So much historical fiction and genre fiction is escapist. It's just not working hard enough with the symbols which we're given."

Although he acknowledges some wonderful works of historical and genre fiction exist, Coupland feels that too much fiction today is about psycho killers and lawyers and people he's never met. "I would love to walk into a bookstore and find books set in the here and now."

Coupland is dedicated to a kind of agnostic spiritual quest. When I ask him where he stands on God, he says he's getting somewhere with the idea. He's finding some personal "syzygy," starting to realize how his life is aligning and where it's going. But he doesn't want to try to spell it all out at this point, and he certainly doesn't want to pontificate. "Somebody who thinks they've found some miracle truth is de facto cattle-blinded," he says intensely. "They've just stopped being curious. That's the scary thing. With them, it's 'Don't question me. Don't talk with me. Because I've got the truth.' I can't imagine life without curiosity."

We order a second beer. When I tell him that some philosophers, such as Charles Hartshorne, and even Christian thinkers such as John Cobb, see creative transformation, which grows out of curiosity and openness, as the essence of life, he says, "I would agree. But what does that have to do with the church, just out of curiosity?"

Some theologians and Bible scholars, I say, believe Jesus' most remarkable trait was his ability to transform people creatively by lovingly breaking down old ways of thinking and offering better possibilities.

Coupland seems to like the idea that faith is more like trust in a process than it is adhering to a dogma. "I mean," he says, "Stalin had answers, didn't he?"

His own thirst for fresh understanding is part of the reason he usually avoids interviews. He can't stand most journalists' cynicism. "You can just see in their eyes the sort of religious fervor of, you know: 'I believe in nothing.' It's a very frightening thing to look into. And why on earth would you want to be complicit in fostering that worldview?"

Coupland is wary about people, and prone to deep depressions — which he describes as sometimes hovering around his head like bug spray for months on end. People in his life, Coupland says, have betrayed him for the most petty of things. Although he won't divulge what the acts were, he says he sometimes wishes the betrayals were bigger, in which case he could understand them better.

One of the few people he trusts is former *Vancouver Magazine* and *Vista* magazine editor Malcolm Parry, now with the *Vancouver Sun*, who gave him a forum in the late 1980s as he shifted from sculpting to writing. He refuses to provide any detail about what he's working on next because he doesn't want to "jinx" it — a view he admits is plain old superstition.

One wonders if Coupland is talking about himself when he says too many people who are loving end up isolated today. "It's like someone's really lonely, and they really have a lot of love to give," he says tenderly. "And they want to fall in love and they want to share it with someone. But no one's taking. There's all this thwarted kindness in the world, which may well be reaching some sort of critical point."

He feels we desperately need ways — "beyond something short-term and palliative like a quick donation to the United Way" — to allow people to express kindness in a consistent way.

He almost sounds as if he'd like to start a new religion. "It really scares me sometimes how few outlets and how few opportunities we have in everyday life, in Western culture generally, to be kind. I think our systems — political and theological and economic — all work together now to make for a world that's not too conducive to kindness. We need to come up with some sort of self-maintaining system of thought that allows people to be better people to other people," he says with a mixture of passion and wistfulness reminiscent of the idealism of his narrator in *Life After God*. Dusk settles in on the mountains and sea and lights start to glow on the ferries. The music and laughter in the bar are rising to a din.

"You can't just leave the world. You can't just kill yourself. That's not an option. So you have to change it." An edge of hurt tinges his voice; he seems to realize he sounds naïvely hopeful. But he's thought about that. "You need," he says, "to make your goals big and broad enough that they never become answered prayers and boomerang around to curse you. I know a lot of people who, you know, worked very hard to get something that they wanted and then they got it. And they were left bereft. Instead, kindness seems to me to be the core of everything."

Coupland tells a story about meeting a "real angel" when, at Chicago's O'Hare airport, on the way home from Europe, he ordered a pizza and then discovered he had only Canadian money in his pocket.

"This woman in the lineup said, 'Oh here. Just eat.' And she gave me two bucks. She said, 'Someone did that for me once.' And she left. Wouldn't it be great if we could go through every day of our lives, like, every moment, being able to exercise that same sort of kindness? That would be heaven, wouldn't it?"

The

New Ancients

For nothing worthy proving can be proven/Nor yet disproven;
wherefore thou be wise/Cleave ever to the sunnier side of doubt/
And cling to Faith beyond the forms of Faith.
— ALFRED, LORD TENNYSON

Bruce Cockburn

"There are no rules. This is what gets me in trouble with certain members of the Christian community. I really don't think it's about rules."

Near the end of our long conversation, Bruce Cockburn suddenly leans over and pulls a New Testament out of his black satchel. The brown-green cover of the Bible has a camouflage design suitable for guerrilla warriors; Cockburn explains he couldn't resist it when he saw it in a U.S. Cavalry mail-order catalogue.

This legendary Canadian performer, one of the very few rockers who count themselves as Christians, rarely talks about his faith today because there is so much potential for misunderstanding. He fears the word "Christianity" now has too many twisted, televangelistic, right-wing connotations. As he checks a passage about love from the Gospel of John, he seems shy about what stereotypes people may have about a guy who carries around a Bible.

Although Cockburn has rarely attended church in the past decade, Christianity has carried him through a career in which he's sold millions of copics of his twenty-two wide-ranging, passionate, tender, poetic, political, spiritual albums. He's won ten Juno awards, played at one of President Bill Clinton's inaugural balls, and received widespread acclaim throughout North America.

To draw attention to issues that he sometimes calls "lost causes" — from clear-cutting forests to the ozone layer, from gay rights to unexploded land mines — Cockburn has traveled widely to troubled lands and taken numerous public stands. The pleasant jazz music and linen tablecloths of this Vancouver restaurant, where Cockburn wears black boots, a black leather jacket, and earrings, contrast sharply with his surroundings on a recent fact-finding trip to Mozambique, where he was in serious fear of being maimed. Cockburn has made several similar trips on behalf of a Canadian-Mozambique coalition called Cocamo. He's helping the group publicize the dangers of the two million abandoned land mines that plague the poverty-stricken country.

One or two such issues usually finds its way into each album of his. His fans love it. But he pays for it when critics or comedians, most recently those from *This Hour Has 22 Minutes*, lampoon him as a buck-toothed soldier of the politically correct.

Whether one agrees with Cockburn, it's impossible to deny that his moral vision comes from a deep and lasting source. His passion for social justice is fueled not by the fashion of the day but by his humble, evolving, non-rule-bound Christianity. In the song "Shipwrecked at the Stable Door," he builds on the theme of Jesus' Sermon on the Mount, that the poor in spirit are blessed, adding, "For theirs shall be the kingdom that the powermongers seek."

In this era when many cynical musicians (and more than a few of the rest of us) sacrifice values for the sake of career success, Cockburn still stands for something beyond his own comfort and glory. He knows he can sound too earnest, but he is consciously using what he believes are his God-given abilities to do something for the world's victims, whether they're North Americans who lose their jobs because of free trade or Latin Americans who lose their lives because of oppression.

He's nobody's person but his own. He's trying to be nobody's person but God's.

Cockburn finds he is not considered politically correct in any camp. Many Christians can't stand his politics; and many political radicals can't stand his Christianity. Even some progressive Christians have trouble with the way, for example, he refers to God as "He." Others are disappointed that he rejects pacifism. An expert marksman and a weapons aficionado, he ruffled more than a few feathers with a famous lyric about how, if he had a rocket launcher, he would use it to blow up Latin American death dealers.

He doesn't have the right to stand idly by if he can stop a loved one, or someone else, from being killed. He speaks softly but decisively, alternating between blunt denunciations and quiet self-deprecation. To Cockburn, following God and Jesus at times means something other than being a meek Christian, especially in the face of corruption, repression, and torture. Like Latin American liberation theologians, who cite the gospel passage about Jesus overturning the tables of the moneychangers to justify their crusades for the poor against dictatorships, Cockburn is not afraid of civil disobedience. He aims his righteous anger against oppressive systems, not individuals.

"The exploitation of child prostitutes makes me angry, for example. I can't do anything about that right now, sitting here. But the time may come when I can do something about it. Hopefully it won't be lobbing a grenade in the window of a porno parlor. But it could be," he says, matter-of-factly. "You know, anything's possible. There are no rules. This is what gets me in trouble with certain members of the Christian community. I really don't think it's about rules."

He acknowledges the existence of "codes of behavior" that help humans get along with each other. But when it comes to finding one's true place in the universe, sometimes you have to act in a way that seems outrageous. "I think it's wrong to ignore what's going on around you. We purport to believe in the concept of loving your brother, which we're told in the Bible is everybody. And I don't see how you can sit and think you're loving your brother when your brother is starving to death or killing his brother or keeping his wife behind a veil. That seems unfair to me. Some of these things touch me for some reasons. I couldn't tell you why, without psychoanalysis. But for some reason the abuse of human dignity is something that matters to me. I abhor it."

When he was a youngster, Cockburn's conservative parents, even though they were agnostics, compelled him to attend Westboro United Church in Ottawa. "The experience wasn't really a spiritual involvement, except kind of accidentally." However, the church's organist encouraged him to write his own compositions, including a jazz service. Cockburn drifted away from church in his teens and didn't return until his late twenties, when circumstance, which he is inclined to spell with a big "C," led him to St. George's Anglican Church in Ottawa.

The church was a hodgepodge of refugee Catholics, West Indians, and prisoners on parole. "The spirit was very alive and very viable in that place — not every time you went, but enough times to remind you what it was. And I've never found another church like that, although I can't say I've honestly made an exhaustive search. I feel if a church wasn't really being offered to me, it probably wasn't necessary. And I feel that way about a lot of stuff."

The closest thing he now has to a faith community is the Greenbelt music festival in England, a non-pious, non-evangelistic Christian festival he says you're never likely to see in North America. Cockburn feels sustained and inspired by his fellow alternative Christian performers there.

These days he acknowledges receiving as much guidance from the world and the people around him, including the non-Christian woman with whom he lives, as he does from the Bible. He only reads his camouflage-design New Testament off and on, "sometimes because I have a burning need for it to tell me something, and other times because I'm bored stiff."

But he prays constantly. Prayer for him is a kind of ongoing conversation with God in which he keeps before his mind's eye the phrase "Your will be done" from the Lord's Prayer. He tries to submit to the will of God. The trick, however, is discerning what God's will is. "If I don't get a gut reaction, then I just wait in as calm and quiet a state as possible. Sometimes you wait a long time. But part of the waiting is trusting that God is part of the process."

It's a tough trust. In Mozambique, two police officers stopped him in front of his hotel and threatened to pull out his fingernails and castrate him if he didn't hand over his money. He handed over the money. At the same time, he silently repeated a mantra he had kept in mind during his stay in the chaotic country: "Total trust. Total trust."

Cockburn's trust in divine providence is embedded in his soul. But his doctrine is hard to pin down in a neat way. This elusiveness is characteristic of a mystic. He follows what he believes God puts before him, no matter whom it displeases or how uncomfortable it may make him. At some point, he believes, trusting in divine providence and following what God puts before him could lead to his death.

Such is the depth of Cockburn's commitment to his God, whom he describes in abstract, philosophical terms. His understanding of the divine has been shaped by an eclectic group of thinkers (many of whom he learned about through books sent by fans): author C. S. Lewis, Catholic process theologian Pierre Teilhard de Chardin, Canadian Jungian analyst Marion Woodman, and St. Francis of Assisi, "the patron saint of the good guys."

Asked about the theological significance of his song "The Gift," in which he sings "everything is motion, to the motion be true," he confirms that he shares Teilhard de Chardin's idea that motion is the essence of life. "Whether you're looking at subatomic particles or at the regeneration of life, you're looking at the need of the universe to move forward. Perhaps it's fanciful to call it forward or backward, but there is that invisible motion that's central to existence. And it might even be true to say that is what God is, although I wouldn't necessarily say that."

Cockburn thinks it's unnecessary to define God precisely. "For me it's just important to feel that I'm part of a process, and that process exists because of God. And it's a process in which God can take a hand any time he wants, and presumably does. What's important for me to remember is that the process is there, even at times when you think it's not or when you've done something totally wrong and there's no recovery from it. But that process is sort of what forgiveness is about. The process is redemptive, even when you lose sight of it."

At this point, Cockburn apologizes for his vagueness. In fact, however, his cosmology grows out of a very learned, informed approach to the world — an approach he often downplays by claiming how little he knows about things he actually knows a lot about, from plastic explosives and the Bible to the destructive policies of the International Monetary Fund.

Despite taking strong stands, Cockburn tries to avoid being self-righteous. Divorced, with a daughter approaching the age of twenty, he is honest enough to acknowledge that part of his penchant for public crusades probably comes from an awkwardness in personal relationships. "You've got to go with what you're good at. I have an easier time relating to people at a distance than to people up close, I guess." He is quite aware that his name gets attention for various causes that might otherwise go unnoticed in North America.

While he admires musicians who he thinks put their money where their mouth is, such as Jackson Browne and Neil Young, he tries to avoid judging the majority of musicians — and other people — who couldn't care less about what happens to the world. In "Tie Me at the Crossroads," he chides himself for his tendency to give free advice like a back-seat driver.

Millions of his fans applaud him for offering advice to the world. Those who do not will simply have to get used to it; Cockburn will be preaching until the day he dies.

Lynn Johnston

*"I don't want a God who is a parent
who might kick me out of the house."*

Lynn Johnston and her family have made their home since 1984 in easygoing countryside where, when you drive by, people wave. The Canadian creator of one of North America's most famous comic strips, *For Better or For Worse*, lives in a big log house that feels, in a casual sort of way, palatial. The tracks for a miniature train, which Johnston's dentist husband of more than twenty years, Rod, sometimes straddles to ride, weave through their large hobby farm on the edge of Trout

Lake, four hours' drive north of Toronto near North Bay.

On the surface, Johnston's life seems idyllically comfortable. But things have been neither easy nor safe for her. Johnston's willingness to recognize difficulty, to dig into the good, bad, and ugly moments of domesticity, is the secret of her phenomenal appeal. Through her strip, she draws together tens of millions of North Americans — moms, dads, kids, grandparents, and singles — by exploring the beauty and tension in everyday family life.

The ethics of a wholesome rebel shine through in her strip, which appears in more than 1,700 newspapers. "From a solid start as a likable family sitcom, *For Better or For Worse* has become, alongside *Doonesbury*, the hardest-hitting strip on the block — and like *Doonesbury*, it has done so without sacrificing wit," said the *New York Daily News*.

Loosely based on the trials and successes of her own family, which includes Aaron, born in 1973 during her first marriage, and Katie, who is in her late teens (the baby of the strip, April, is born of Johnston's imagination), *For Better or For Worse* doesn't elicit big yucks as much as it does smiling nods of insight. Johnston quietly challenges readers by being herself: an imaginative person who embraces different people and ideas.

Along with tales about raising babies, attending high-school graduations, sending teenage kids off to summer jobs, and the death of the family dog, Farley (named after Farley Mowat, who has *For Better or For Worse* strips about Farley tacked on the wall of his Nova Scotia bathroom), Johnston's strip tells the stories of outsiders. A wheelchair-bound teacher appears as a regular character. She has also portrayed a boy who feared beatings by his dad, a baby born with six fingers, and, most controversially, a teenager struggling to accept his homosexuality.

After offering lunch in her sunny kitchen, Johnston sits down at her pine table with the old spaniel, Willie, at her feet, and talks in a warm, confessional way about her family, the world, and her searching Christianity.

In the 1950s, she used to pray she'd marry a clergyman. That way, she fantasized, she could ghostwrite happier sermons than those she endured at St. John's Anglican Church in North Vancouver, where she was exposed to guilt trips early and often. "The priest used to make you feel as if you personally had nailed Jesus to the cross. He left you feeling so much a sinner, so fearful of God." She admits she wasn't the easiest kid to put up with, always playing the rowdy clown in the choir. "I acted out because I thought I was fat and ugly," she says. "I knew I was smart and talented, but I considered myself cloddish."

Of course, self-esteem often has little to do with reality. Photos from Johnston's early twenties reveal her as a fetching, slim woman. Now approaching her fifties, with wavy hair and a touch of makeup, she has kept herself fit and robust.

As a preteen, Johnston left grim St. John's and on her own attended a nearby, upbeat United Church, St. Andrew's. "I loved the United Church. I loved the smell of it." But she began questioning her faith in God when her childhood friend, Elly Jansen, died of cancer. "Although I professed to have abandoned my faith, I wrote long, heartfelt letters to Elly and burned them, hoping she'd read the phantom thoughts and forgive me for not knowing how seriously ill she was; for not being there when she died."

Nevertheless, Johnston kept singing in the church choir, until one day, as sixteen-year-old Johnston took off her choir vestment after a service, a fellow choir member — a man in his fifties — came up behind her and grabbed her breasts. He was pretending to help remove her cassock, "but he was really giving me a damn good feel," she says, still indignant. The congregation respected the man, and in those pre-sex-abuse-awareness days, Johnston dared not tell anyone.

She left the church and didn't return for almost two decades. In the meantime, she went to a Vancouver art school, got married too early, had Aaron, and divorced. It was not until the early 1980s, while living in Lynn Lake, a remote Prairie mining town 685 miles north of Winnipeg with Rod, who had to fly to reach his patients, that Johnston dared venture back to the church.

She became heavily involved in an Anglican parish where a priest delivered affection-filled sermons. But eventually she left again, this time because she tired of struggling with the church board over petty issues such as what color to paint the church.

Since moving to northern Ontario in 1984, Johnston has occasionally attended the United Church in the nearby village of Corbeil, where her brother-in-law, who is gay and living with a long-term male partner, is the music director.

"Generally, people who go to church have strong morals and are just and fair," she says, as comfortably as if she were chatting with a friend. "But I don't like the word 'Christ.' I believe very strongly Jesus was probably one of the most important teachers the world will ever produce." But the early church fathers, she believes, probably made a mistake when they declared Jesus the one and only son of God. She joins those who see the claim that Jesus is the one Lord and Savior as a barrier to Christian faith. "I'm starting to see other people as divine too — such as saints and exceptional people."

Although her beliefs about Jesus may outrage some traditional Christians, Johnston's ideas are not that radical. She has the support of many New Testament scholars and Christian theologians, including many in the United Church of Canada and some American mainstream denominations. In her book *A History of God*, religious historian Karen Armstrong writes about how the early apostles never considered Jesus the incarnation of God himself. When they called Jesus "the son of God," they meant it the way early Jews did. It was a way of expressing Jesus' intimacy with God. "Paul meant that Jesus simply possessed God's powers and Spirit, which manifested God's activity on earth and were not to be identified with the inaccessible divine essence," Armstrong writes. "Not surprisingly, in the Gentile world, the new Christian did not always retain the sense of these subtle distinctions, so that eventually Jesus, a man who had stressed his weak, mortal humanity was believed to have been divine."

Similarly, Johnston rejects the notion of a fearsome God. "I believe, through Jesus' teaching, we can discover a loving God, a caring God, an accepting God. The Christian God accepts everyone. I don't want a God who is a parent who might kick me out of the house. I don't want an elite club."

Like some other disillusioned Christians, in her younger days Johnston seriously considered converting to Judaism, and she still admires the Jewish tradition. However, when some Jewish people once gave her the feeling she would be securing membership in a private group, she didn't like the sense of exclusiveness.

Johnston's "peoplevert" personality and sense of open-armed inclusiveness received a shock when a gay friend was murdered several years ago. The event prompted her to introduce a gay teenage character into her strip, causing a North American furor.

After that series of strips ran, she received hundreds of brutal letters, some filled with filthy language. About a dozen newspapers cancelled the strip. She gained new fans, but lost some old ones. It hurt. "I didn't know the consequences would be as violent and long-lasting as they have been."

Johnston won't, however, be worn down. "It's still a wholesome strip," she insists. She compares fighting anti-gay attitudes to fighting apartheid; she's in it for the long term. Her husband was one of the first dentists who would treat people with AIDS.

The family helps those who are struggling in many other ways. Johnston supports the local United Church's food bank. She and Rod also single-handedly finance an American Medical Missions Association program that schools and feeds 128 children a day in Honduras. Johnston has many disabled friends and supports Easter Seals' programs for disabled children.

The habit of embracing people who are different comes in part from growing up in a strict, British-bred family where outsiders were not embraced, explains Johnston. "I've always been defying my parents by getting to know people who are different." This quality of embodying God by being open to all is one shared by Jesus, who challenged authority and hung out with the outcasts of ancient society: low-class women, tax collectors for the Roman occupiers, and children.

Although rebelling against her late parents may have taught Johnston about being open and inclusive, it also caused pain. She kept her distance from her parents. And sometimes she felt like a terrible mother herself, screaming in desperation at her kids when they were young. The Johnstons have been in family therapy. Johnston believes in giving children firm guidelines and tough love. She hopes she's created the opposite of the family in which she was raised, where her parents, although they had many good qualities, rarely expressed anger, warmth, or other emotions directly. "I had tremendous respect for my parents, but I didn't have that spiritual love for them that a kid should have."

But relationships with parents are complex and multifaceted. Sitting at her kitchen table, Johnston tells a story of her mother's death a few years back. She helped cross her mother's still-warm hands over her dead body. She recalls how her father sat down beside the deathbed and talked to his wife's body for the longest time.

She was moved. "I just thought, 'Oh. To have been so loved.'" Johnston grows silent and her eyes fill with tears. She looks out her kitchen window at the rustling cottonwoods and the birds fluttering near the birdfeeder.

So open is she about her emotions, to whatever possibility is present in each moment, that she does not try to stop crying in front of me, a virtual stranger. When she speaks again, she explains that part of her sorrow over her mother's death comes from the feeling that her mother had never been fulfilled. She may not have bubbled over with affection, but she was highly intelligent. She taught her kids Latin and introduced them to a new word each week. She had wanted to be a doctor, but in her day, British women had rarely been permitted an advanced education.

Since her mother's death, Johnston has felt the urge to bond with her in some way. And one day she did. Swimming in her indoor pool, Johnston suddenly sensed her mother sitting on the pool stairwell. When she looked down at her own hands, she saw instead her mother's. "We came to terms," she says simply. It was gratifying.

Johnston has experienced paranormal moments before, including one fairly disturbing one. She was walking through her kitchen one day when she had a powerful feeling about one of her old friends. "I thought I should call him." Johnston later found out that just at the time she had felt compelled to contact her friend, who was gay, he had been murdered; his throat had been slit by an acquaintance he had tried to help.

Such psychic experiences are part of a long journey Johnston has been on since her teenage years, when Elly died and she thought she had lost all her faith. She began contemplating spirituality again and returned to church in the 1980s because of an experience she had at

Hamilton's McMaster University in the 1970s that restored her belief in life after death.

A medical illustrator, Johnston was watching her first autopsy. Seeing the surgical dissection of a woman's body overwhelmed her not with revulsion, but with awe. Instead of throwing up as many people do, Johnston remembers inhaling the gases from the woman's syphilitic body and the odor of formaldehyde. She revels in the details: "When they opened up the woman's brain, I expected it to be wonderful. But it was just like hamburger. I began realizing the body is like a television set, a maze of intricate wires and parts. But as I held this woman's brain in my hands, feeling detached and technical, suddenly there was this feeling of miracle. I realized a soul, a spirit, gives a person feelings and mind. My belief in God suddenly returned. I put my arms around the doctor's neck and left the autopsy room. He knew what I was feeling."

Johnston favors the idea of reincarnation, which may not be as heretical as many traditional Christians believe. Many scholars say reincarnation was a common belief among Greeks around the time of Jesus, but was eventually rejected by the early church fathers who created the Christian canon. "I believe we're given a body and soul and the choice between right and wrong — between greed and giving, between love and lust. You get points for learning. Then, in death, there's a period of time in which you review the life you led. And the lessons you failed to learn in your past, you may have to learn again. This is one heck of a video game we're in. To me, the ultimate reason for life is to learn and to perfect, so you're able to come back many times to learn something more. Maybe the belief is just the product of my vivid imagination, but it's my fervent hope."

As she walks to the kitchen to get some more coffee, she says casually, that she would really like to meet Jesus in another life. "I'd love to get his views on this religion that's been set up in his name. I'd like to ask him if he ever would have believed it could have gone so far. I'd ask him if he likes being so deified, so loved, so worshipped. I hope he'd say 'No.'"

With only a hint of a smile, she adds: "Of course I'd have to learn Aramaic."

Susan Aglukark

IAN LINDSAY

"I'm weak on my own. I think everybody is."

Her Inuit grandmother died drunk on the Arctic ice. A brother and sister attempted suicide. A close friend killed herself. She was molested when she was nine. Her Inuit name is Uuliniq, which means "scarred from burns." Yet tiny singer Susan Aglukark has done more than survive. She has become a Canadian icon, winning numerous Juno awards and nominations for her original blends of pop and aboriginal music. The *New York Times* calls her an "international star."

As she talks, the whites of her Inuk eyes gleam as fresh as snow. She seems, I suggest, to be one of those unusual resilient types who would never contemplate suicide, whatever the pressure.

She replies, "Uh, you'd be wrong."

Her voice is not heavy when she confides. It is almost teasing: the frank approach of a woman for whom suffering has always clung too close in the barren lands of the Northwest Territories. "I've reached a low point in my life. I think everybody has. And for the briefest of seconds I've considered suicide." She was thirteen or fourteen, she says, glancing down at her lap in the noisy Hotel Vancouver restaurant.

Her brown eyes moisten under her short, boyish haircut. The only thing that has allowed her to survive, she says, is God. "I'm weak on my own. I think everybody is." Suddenly, as is often the way with people who have known real suffering, Aglukark bounces out of seriousness. She jokes that her friend, Buffy St. Marie, the native Indian singer who wrote "Universal Soldier" and other hit songs, seems a hardy exception to the rule that all people are weak on their own.

Aglukark's life is testimony to the spiritual power of the Arctic. Whites from southern Canada and the United States, including authors Timothy Findley and Barry Lopez, join her in finding the chilling, awesome far north a kind of cathedral. But too many other whites romanticize the Inuit and the exotic image of a nature-oriented, shamanistic spirituality. Most whites don't realize the shamans had their problems too — notably a tendency toward a kind of religious literalism. Or that most Inuit, if they are religious at all, are Christians.

"I accepted Christ when I was eleven," Aglukark says. "I've never changed. I have no desire to." Her parents are independent evangelical preachers connected to the Arctic missions of the Pentecostal Assemblies of Canada and the Vancouver-based Glad Tidings Church. Growing up along the banks of Hudson Bay in the town of Arviat, population 1,200, Aglukark first sang in churches. Her admiration for her parents' religious dedication shows up in songs such as "Mama's Prayers" and "Dreams for You." Although she has had serious conflicts with her parents and the church, she still maintains that Jesus is her rock.

You can sense her sureness in the way she walks: without urban artifice. In loose blue pants, she treads softly and solidly, the way one must to remain steady crossing Arctic tundra and ice. She is a sturdy woman, unafraid to look into the heart of Arctic darkness and face the horrors among her people. She testified against her molester, a family friend, in 1989 when she heard he was abusing others. In her song, "Anger and Tears," Aglukark tackles child sexual abuse head on: the narrator asks why she wasn't kept safe at night, and when the hurtful memories will stop.

Although Aglukark calls Jesus her "graceful master," she also takes pride in most non-Christian Inuit traditions. Her two big albums, *Arctic Rose* and the top-selling *This Child*, echo with Inuit chants, earthy rhythms, and the Inuktitut language. She has empathy for those who practise traditional Inuit religion, but ultimately she rejects shamanism. "When shamanism was practised, it was all the Inuit knew. We had no choice. My personal opinion is anything aside from Christ, including shamanism, isn't going to save our souls."

She doesn't speak about her faith unless asked. For her, what counts is that forgiveness is the center of Christianity. She finds most humans unforgiving by nature, but has "come to trust that Christ is the very opposite." She has thought and prayed long and hard about forgiveness. She had to — not only to overcome the anger she felt toward those who victimized her and her friends, but to overcome the hell of growing up a preacher's kid.

"Religion played a big role in the deterioration of the parent-children relationship. We didn't have a relationship with our parents. It was just church. You were just expected to be good," she says. Her voice, bell-like and uplifting in song, sounds young in conversation. Her six brothers and sisters endured guilt and constant moral judgment from her parents. They heard of Satan's power to control them. Her parents' high expectations pushed some siblings to rebel and attempt suicide. Others tried, unsuccessfully, to be perfect. "The reactions of the kids went from one extreme to the other. There was no normality."

But glimmers of forgiveness are beginning to break through to Aglukark's extended family. The children are demanding room to make mistakes. "Now my parents are realizing judgment is not the intention of God. To follow Jesus is to follow his teachings and example to the best of your abilities," she says with a smile, pointing her small, thin index fingers into the air for emphasis.

Family guilt was not the only curse of being raised by evangelical preachers in the far north. Ridicule was another.

Evangelical Christians were a rarity in the North in her early days. Most Inuit were Catholic or Anglican or nothing. Shamanism, if it was practised at all, was underground. When her father converted from Anglicanism to charismatic Pentecostalism, the neighbors were far from accepting. "We were called holy rollers all our lives. People would say, 'Here come the Hallelulahs.'"

Susan's mother, especially, tried to shield the kids from the worst insults. But they couldn't help but be caught in the crossfire. Aglukark was a shy girl and sometimes Inuit kids spat at her and her siblings. "They were just kids. They didn't understand. We didn't blame them. But it does carry emotional scars that we are just now dealing with."

In the end, she believes all the struggles helped make her strong and able to stand up for what she believes — even to face those within her own faith who condemn her. Although most evangelical Christians accept and celebrate her Christian witness, some remain severe critics. "Secular people never attack me. But some Christians, some churches, some Christian media are the most judgmental." They claim, she says, that a Christian shouldn't try to straddle the worlds of born-again belief and secular fame. "But Christ didn't do that. He walked among the pagans. Some Christians want a perfect Christian. But there is none."

There is little reason to fear Aglukark will succumb to debauchery, or to the shallow nihilism and anger pervading much contemporary music and society. She doesn't drink or smoke. When she attends parties with famous musicians, she enjoys them, but always sneaks away early.

"The scriptures keep me grounded. I'm walking a very fine line between the record business and my beliefs. The smallest decision can be very stressful. I have to be careful because I want to get my message out to both Inuit and non-Inuit."

And what is her message? "It's very basic. It's as simple as, 'We're okay. It doesn't matter whether you're aboriginal or not, we're all *okay*.'" She pushes out the last word; she knows how easy it is to feel unworthy.

Yet Aglukark plays down her own suffering. She responds to tragedy by promoting harmony and hope — on both a personal and political level. As a one-time executive assistant for the Inuit Tapirisat lobby group, she believes in the native land-claim process and the hard-won dream of Inuit self-government, which will become a reality in 1999 in a new land called Nunavut. "My dad's been involved with Nunavut since it began. It's one of the most exciting things to happen to the Inuit since first contact with the white man. It's huge. And I really believe the Inuit people are ready to take it on." Her hit song "O Siem," inspired by the Inuit word for the celebration that occurs when different people meet, counters racism and economic division by stressing that everyone is family.

To promote hope, however, Aglukark knows she first has to deal with pain. After performing before young people in the far north, she has stayed up all night talking with them about their struggles with suicide, drugs, and sexual abuse. She cries with them and hugs them. "Almost always what happens is they want to pray. And I will hold their hands, or sit or stand and do that with them. But as a preacher's kid, I've learned never to force Jesus on anyone."

She prays all the time. "It's nothing extraordinary. I can do it right now. It's a constant sort of discussion with God. I don't kneel down much. When a decision comes up, the first thing that comes into my mind is 'Okay God, what now?' That happens thirty to forty times a day. I don't wait for an audible voice to respond. That hardly ever happens. God has given us the knowledge to make the right decision, based on our relationship with Him. If the decision is right, it evolves; if it's wrong, God is there to forgive us."

Prayer, Aglukark believes, gives her access to all the peace, wisdom, and healing in the universe. It is through non-rational means, through feelings and the imagination, that she connects with the immutable force behind the universe. Her friendship with God, however, is sometimes a challenge to maintain in the noisy cities like Toronto where she now spends most of her time. She often yearns to be back among her people, where she feels more comfortable sitting on the floor, sleeping with her sisters, and walking on floors stained with the blood of butchered animals brought home from the hunt.

She has also always loved walking alone on the tundra. "Big barren country doesn't scare me. It's what I crave." The mystical connection happens more naturally when the smell of caribou is on the wind and she is alone on Arctic land that seems to stretch to eternity.

"Because of the openness, the quietness, and the peacefulness, He's a lot clearer out there," she says, smiling. "You know the line from the Bible: 'Be still and know that I am God.'"

Ann Copeland

BILL KEAY

*"The gospel is about trying to incarnate a love
which is both radical and not stupid."*

Ann Copeland was an Ursuline nun for twelve years. She still plays the
organ at her Catholic Church in Sackville, New Brunswick. She values
prayer, transcendence and the sacredness of human relationships. She
has studied the Christian tradition in detail and understands its sub-
tleties and paradoxes.

Perhaps that's why the acclaimed author just can't force herself
to recite the Apostle's Creed every Sunday morning. "I hesitate

to stand up and declare something I may not really, truly, in my heart, believe."

Copeland is the author of *The Golden Thread* (a finalist for Canada's Governor-General's Award for fiction) and *Strange Bodies on a Stranger Shore*, both of which consist of linked stories about a nun. Asked what she can't accept about the Apostle's Creed, the official statement of faith of many churches, Copeland hesitates, then bows her head nearly on to the restaurant table and, murmuring, tries to remember it: "I believe in God, the Father Almighty . . . his only son . . . power of the Holy Spirit . . . sitteth at the right hand of God . . . come to judge the living and the dead . . . the communion of saints . . . the life everlasting . . . ."

Copeland has been feeling flamboyant and playful up to this point. When I tried to find a place in downtown Vancouver to interview her, she joked that we should photograph her in front of the liquor bottles lining the hotel bar. Then she suggested she pose at the hotel piano, because music is important to her. She played a ragtime tune, followed by "Tea for Two." When we finally sat down at a restaurant to talk, she was in such a jolly mood she was reluctant at first to take on the serious business of declaring which orthodox Christian doctrines she doesn't actually believe in. Eventually, however, she takes on the task.

"I believe we are creations of a loving God, but I don't know if Jesus was God. I have to answer that honestly. Actually, it's not a big question in Christianity today. But certainly the gospel is for me important." As she speaks, her punchy black eyebrows under white hair add intensity to her eyes.

Copeland points out the phrases of the creed she does accept. "Hey, by the way, I do believe in the Holy Spirit," she says in a bouncy voice, a big smile creasing her cheeks. "And the communion of saints. Great idea. I talk to them all the time. And life everlasting. I don't necessarily believe in physical resurrection, but I believe there is an immortality connected with what we call the soul."

The mainstream churches are full of active Christians such as Copeland who don't necessarily believe that the essence of Christianity is Jesus' bodily resurrection from the dead. Resurrection stories are relatively common in Indian religions, for example; the risen person is considered holy, but not supernatural or divine. Even to many theologians, physical resurrection is not the key to Christianity.

The question of life after death is open-ended for some who call themselves Christians. To them, life after death remains a hope, rather than a guarantee. For Copeland, however, life after death is a reality. "My husband laughs at me. But I talk to people who have died ahead of me. My mother died this past year. I've talked to her."

Does her much-loved mother answer back? "Oh, no. I don't know how those answers come. I'm sorry. It's just part of being raised in the communion of saints — that notion that these souls are just on the other side of the pale. There is a world we do not see. And there is a spiritual reality we cannot imagine. I believe the dimensions of that world are staggering."

Copeland is a delightful blend of reverence and irreverence. She cracks jokes about my questions. "C'mon, Doug, ask a better one than that," she teases. She makes up some of her own. She hypothesizes that it would be great to be a religion writer.

The central character in some of her writing, a nun named Claire Delaney, sometimes speaks of striving to have no desire for worldly things; Copeland also believes it's worthwhile to be detached from material possessions. "But I'm beset by contradictions," she says, touching her dangling earrings. "I could walk into Holt Renfrew and want the whole rack. Let's not erase desire completely." Asked about the subtle humor that pops up in her stories, she says, "I think that

God has a sense of humor. And if we didn't have one, why wouldn't we just slit our wrists?"

Growing up in New England in a devout Catholic family, she was swept up by the openness and ecumenicism of the Vatican II era. When she was young, she wanted to be a saint. So she entered the Ursuline order, studied literature, eventually obtained a Ph.D. and ended up teaching at Indiana State University. Convent rules included: no movies; no television; and no talking to men unless absolutely necessary. "I matriculated," says Copeland, "at the university of sainthood."

After many years of internal struggle, she left the order when she concluded it showed no real commitment to true, open, intellectual pursuit. She married a literature professor, who rarely attends church and finds the mass "a strange Byzantine rite," and moved twenty years ago to Sackville, where she attends a rural parish. If her beloved parish wasn't there, she could imagine not attending any church. She would not listen to "any old jerk" go on about the Bible.

Many of Copeland's stories feature the character of Claire Delaney, who became a nun, left the convent, and became a mother of two. Copeland, who has two sons in their twenties, doesn't hide the fact that Delaney's life is loosely based on her own.

The Delaney stories raise no direct quarrel with spirituality, or even with the church. They offer bold, sensual, perceptive insights into life within and without the convent: forbidden relationships; rustling habits; and the metaphysical complexities of losing one's life in order to find it. The *New York Times* calls the stories "intelligent and beautiful."

I ask if Copeland is willing to comment on some of the stumbling blocks many people find in Catholic doctrine. She readily agrees.

Should women be allowed to be priests?

"Absolutely. I have no patience at all with those who say there is a crisis of a shortage of priests. And priests who have married, who have served the church so devotedly and still wish to, should also be allowed to remain priests."

Artificial contraception?

"It's absurd," she says, "to make a big distinction between artificial and natural contraception."

Abortion?

"It's troubling. I would not absolutely ban abortion. I've known too many people who have agonized through a decision over it." She wonders, though, whether mass culture is bombarding us with the message that sex is cheap and abortions should be easy. "Attitudes like that can brutalize relationships between men and women."

She also wants to clarify that, despite her questions about the creed, there are wonderful things about the Catholic tradition and being a nun. She cherished communal life and contrasts it with the what's-in-it-for-me attitude of secularism. "The sharing of common experience with a group of people who were exceptionally fine — I've never had that duplicated anywhere."

Catholic tradition is bred in her bones. But instead of leaving Copeland with unassailable doctrine, it has given her a profound sense of transcendence. Copeland firmly believes in the power of transcendence. "I think there are moments in your life when you experience a sense of higher reality. Music is a very important meeting place for me of passion and transcendence. But it can also come through reading literature, sex, an extraordinary meeting with another person, or religious ritual."

Prayer is also a key route to transcendence. "I talk to God all the time — walking down the street, anywhere. I know that sounds pretentious, but I don't mean it that way." God is present right now, in this conversation, she says. God is also present when her congregation gathers at the Communion table "to hear the word, to listen for what meaning it might make."

Although she does not believe in bodily resurrection (she's going to be cremated), she is drawn to the nobility in the story of Jesus' crucifixion and resurrection, as well as the wonderful accounts of his spiritual appearances to the apostles. One of her favorite phrases from the gospels is about taking risks: "Launch out into the deep." This was Jesus' advice to the apostles when they couldn't catch fish. "That speaks to me about love and life. To me it means, 'Don't be afraid. And don't stop too soon.'"

Another Biblical phrase came to Copeland during a time of despair. Her spirituality calls her to be open to others, an attitude that is the essence, according to Christian theologian John Cobb, of the divine process of creative transformation. So she found it especially painful when, despite the love she lavished on him, her adopted baby son never seemed to relate to her. Only years later did she and her husband discover that little Andrew suffered from fetal-alcohol syndrome.

"I'm going to tell you a great moment of grace I had in connection with Andrew, which I've never talked about, except with my husband," she says. "Andrew and I had very limited emotional connection. And that was exhausting for me, because I like to connect to another human being at the deepest level. My question had become: 'Is our task as parents to be nurturing, or custodial?' In the middle of the night, when he was about fifteen, I went downstairs, and I was sitting, probably praying in some vague way, and [Jesus' words] came to me: 'When I was in prison, you visited me. When I was naked, you clothed me.' All of a sudden I just thought: this is not a nifty relationship. In other words, it was custodial. It sounds simplistic, but it was a very religious moment for me."

Perhaps loved ones of those with disabilities can understand

Copeland's epiphany — the sense of spiritual liberation that did not make her meaner. After the revelation, Copeland and her husband decided to send Andrew to a group home in Nova Scotia. "It is a very special, loving place." They still see him, of course, "but he has very little sustained memory. He only lives in the bubble of the present."

Despite her non-doctrinaire approach, Copeland still finds the central theme for her ebullient life in the New Testament. "The gospel," she says, " is about trying to incarnate a love which is both radical and not stupid."

Tony Hillerman

*"I'm not here just to while away the time.
And it's a waste of time to just chase money."*

When the land mine exploded under him, Tony Hillerman thought his life was over. "I was layin' there with both legs broken and I was blinded. And I was thinkin', 'It's soaking wet, and I'm cold. I think I'm dying.' And I got this wonderful warm feeling of 'Boy, what a relief.'" Hillerman was behind Nazi lines, with most of his troop already dead. He was nineteen years old. If he'd lost a few more cups of blood, the world would have never known his myth-saturated

122

mysteries, which have sold more than ten million copies to date.

"It's hard to describe," says the author of such books as *Sacred Clowns* and *Coyote Waits*. "It was an ineffable feeling of joy. I just had this feeling that I'd passed muster, that I'd run the course and it was going to be great. I hadn't had the guts to do anything very bad in my life — one thing about being raised a strict Catholic is you have a solid guilt complex. So I felt like I was being welcomed. I thought, 'This pretty well proves that I'm all right, doesn't it?'"

But somebody called a temporary truce to deal with all the wounded. A jeep hauled Hillerman out, and he ended the Second World War with a couple of hero's medals on his chest. He still remembers feeling "sort of disappointed."

But the near-death experience strengthened Hillerman's faith, which had been weakening ever since he'd left behind his Catholic roots in Oklahoma for the army's profane ranks.

Telling the war story across a table during a visit to Vancouver, Hillerman, in his late sixties, seems far removed from his mysteries' main characters: two native cops, Lt. Joe Leaphorn and Officer Jim Chee, who ply their trade among the sacred land of the Navajo and Hopi Indians. Except for his lyrical southwestern drawl, Hillerman doesn't seem like the rugged western type. Rather, his manner evokes the root meaning of the word "courtly." He is affable, dignified, and polite. With his vaguely Prince-Valiant-style haircut and his pronounced jowls, he looks like medieval German royalty.

Despite Hillerman's European appearance, the desert, canyons, mesa, and sky of Arizona and New Mexico run thick in his veins. He is the only white man ever to receive an award from the Navajo, the biggest tribe in the United States, as a "Friend of the Dineh (Navajo)." His twelve mystery novels, with evocative titles such as *Dance Hall of the Dead*, *A Thief of Time*, and *Skinwalkers*, reveal a deep understanding of the many facets of contemporary Navajo and Hopi culture: computers and shamanism, land developers and burial grounds, alcoholism and millenia-old tradition.

Yet, he is not an Indian "wannabe." Navajo leaders, says Hillerman, seem to respect the fact that he is a practising Catholic — a former altar boy who took church seriously when he was a kid. ("Common sense had told me you had to have a Creator.") He now attends 8,000-member Annunciation parish in Albuquerque, New Mexico.

Astounding book sales, and deals for upcoming movies, have come his way even though he works the fringe of the mystery genre. Suffused with spiritual and ethical themes, his stories contain precious little sex, money, or violence. Said a *New York Times* reviewer: "He may be the only writer who has been compared to both Raymond Chandler and Carlos Castaneda."

Hillerman's novels follow the college-educated Chee and Leaphorn as they try to solve crimes against backdrops of witchcraft, 7-Elevens, healing rituals, native militancy, turquoise talismens, insensitive archeologists, family lineages, and an inspiring landscape. *Sacred Clowns*, for example, centers on the investigation of the murder of an Indian who performs the role of a Koshare comic figure; it shows how traditional Navajo ethics are based on laughing at human imperfection. The title of *Talking God* is derived from a Navajo rite in which several gods, or *yeis*, are called upon to cure a serious illness. The book's real focus, however, is on the dubious scientific practice of collecting the skeletons of long-dead people for museum displays. *Listening Woman* is about Navajo religious figures who represent human intelligence and aggressiveness.

The native religious sensibility Hillerman blends into his mysteries avoids fundamentalism; instead it builds on an understanding of myth similar to that of the well-known twentieth-century religion specialist

Joseph Campbell. "Mythology is the way we try to understand the ineffable. It drives you beyond language and into the realm of poetry," Hillerman says. He leans forward in his chair, determined to make the point clearly. "Do I believe the book of Genesis? Let's face it, it's metaphor. It's beautiful. But I can't believe man has existed on this planet 5,218 years — and descended from Adam and Eve — except in a metaphorical, symbolic, poetic way."

As a Christian, Hillerman finds in the life and teachings of Jesus the key to the nature of the Creator. "The message of Jesus is: 'God loves you guys, and he expects you to love one another, to treat each other with gentility and care.' Christ taught us we are the children of God." We are made in God's image, he says. That doesn't mean God is human. It means humans are like God intellectually. "God is a kind of intelligence."

Although Hillerman is highly devout, like most North American Catholics, he is theologically liberal. In his parish, against Catholic discipline, girls are allowed, as they are in many parishes, to read the liturgy and help serve mass. "Women keep the church alive, for heaven's sake. The Pope may have to excommunicate us all," he says with a smile.

The fact is, he says, most North American Catholics are like him and the people at his church. "We're not as authoritarian as the traditionalists would want, but we are the church. We are the faithful." He is moved when the faithful gather for the central Christian ritual of communion, in which they symbolically ingest the blood and body of Jesus Christ. "At the communion of all these friends and neighbors and the Lord, you look around and you see all these really good people: people who are getting up early, going out and visiting the old people, visiting the sick, visiting people in jail and working at the homeless shelters. That's the church in action."

How would he like to see the church hierarchy change? For starters, he'd like to de-emphasize sex. He regrets how Christianity has become obsessed with sex. "You can read the gospels until your heart's content and you'll find the good Lord was not particularly interested in it. He hardly mentioned it." When the gospels tell of people stoning a woman for adultery, he says, Jesus told them, "Let those who are without sin cast the first stone."

On the other hand, Hillerman agrees that the Pope is right to be worried about moral decadence. Hillerman himself chooses not to describe torrid love scenes in his books because his young daughter might want to read them.

"But if I were Pope, I'd issue a whole flood of encyclicals," he says, spreading his arms, relishing the opportunity to talk about his faith.

"I'd say: 'All right, first, we're going to have married priests. In the second place, we're going to have women priests. Third place: nobody can become a cardinal unless he's married and unless he's raised a couple of kids. And nobody can be a cardinal unless he's been a parish priest in some grungy place.' I'd tell all cardinals: 'Go to Angola, southern Italy, work in a vineyard.' I'd bring in people who had worked in missions in Guatemala, Bangladesh, and Africa and I'd make them cardinals."

Then he would have the world's most incredible garage sale at the Vatican. "I'd clean it out. And all the money would go to feed the starvin' folks." This, he says, would lead to a huge revival of Catholicism. Religion would take off in North America, he is sure, if more Christians would put their money where their faith is — the way the Navajo do.

He's drawn to the steadfast non-materialism of the Navajo. "If you're Navajo and you own too much, you're considered a bad Navajo — because chances are your family is poorer. So the Navajo ask, 'Why haven't you helped your family?'"

You'd never see a Donald Trump or George Steinbrenner rise out of Navajo culture, he says. The Navajo and Hopi are dedicated to helping their community. "Not many people actually let their purported religious beliefs affect the way they live. But the Navajo and the Hopi do. When you see them, man, all of a sudden you feel like you're faced with a whole bunch of people whose faith is so strong." Hillerman tells the story of a Navajo man who strove hard to get a job as an engineer. But when his relative was killed in a car crash, he was asked to come back home to lead a curing ceremony to bring harmony back to the family. "He told his new boss he had to take off nine days. The boss said he couldn't spare him. So he quit. That impresses the heck out of me."

Hillerman — who has raised six kids, four of whom were adopted — has made a lot of money since he began writing about Chee and Leaphorn more than two decades ago after a journalism career. He and his wife, Marie, have a policy of giving their money away surreptitiously, the way the Bible suggests. "You don't stride up front and make a big deal of your contribution," he says. "Do you want the credit on earth or in heaven?"

Anyway, he says with a smile, it's not that hard to say so long to your earnings these days. "The government has made it much easier to be a good Christian with its new tax laws. I've got to pay a heck of a lot of income tax — 60 percent." But he's not complaining. In fact, Hillerman wouldn't mind seeing the rich taxed more. "I'd like to see an inheritance tax. I don't like the idea of inherited wealth at all. It doesn't do anybody any good. It creates a kind of ruling class — a kind of elite that goes against my populist grain."

Here's a guy who takes his Christianity seriously. Unlike many of the well-off, he doesn't whine about taxes because he thinks governments play a worthwhile role redistributing wealth. He picked up that attitude in part because of his war experience, where he realized God not only loved him, but expected some performance from him. "You know, I'm not here just to while away the time. And it's a waste of time to just chase money. I'm going to do something, for heaven's sake."

He gives of himself because he thinks that was Jesus' main message. "If somebody hits you, turn the other cheek. If somebody wants your coat, give it to him. Be generous. Be kind. If we paid attention to that, we'd have a nice world, wouldn't we?"

Robertson Davies

JEFF VINNICK

"What is it that makes a human being go? It is energy.
And the physicists tell us that energy never vanishes.
So when the body is worn out and dies, where does the energy go?"

The low clouds look wrathful outside the downtown window. In vest and tic, Robertson Davies sits across a round cherrywood table, sharing his wondrous views on spirituality. I flip my tape over and ask why Satan often popped up in his novels.

KRRAAAABOOOOOOOOM!

The sky thunders. The Vancouver Hotel shakes for a few seconds. Then silence.

"You see," says Davies, deeply and slowly.

His eyes light up. In this conversation, which takes place about a year before his death in 1995, Davies' eighty-one-year-old voice is arch. Behind me, his winsome wife, Brenda, knitting on a sofa, says: "You mentioned *him*."

Brenda and I laugh. I ask Davies, an admirer of the great psychologist Carl Jung, if he thinks that the explosion (which I discovered later had been detonated by a film crew) coinciding with the mention of Satan might be an example of synchronicity, a Jungian theory that some concurrent events are mystically significant.

Behind his famous long gray beard, Davies smiles and winks.

What does Davies, one of Canada's foremost men of letters and an internationally acclaimed author, make of Satan?

"Well, the devil is a shorthand term for the evil principle in life. The devil keeps popping up in the funniest places." The author of more than thirty books, whose novels include *Fifth Business*, *Rebel Angels*, and *The Cunning Man*, winner of Canadian and international literary prizes too numerous to mention, goes on to describe two five-year-old boys in Norway who were charged with murdering a baby, as well as the two Liverpool lads convicted of killing young Jamie Bulger. "It certainly seems something was at work there, an evil principle."

He contrasts the way some children of the wealthy turn out loathsome while some acquaintances of his overcame terrible upbringings to become successful benefactors. "Why one and not the other? I don't know. But it's observable that a bad background doesn't necessarily mean a bad outcome." He believes evil is like a force that can act through a person.

Why would some become vulnerable to this evil force?

"I haven't any idea. But you know, it's said in the Bible that some people are tempted and resist, and some people are tempted and don't resist."

Credulity and skepticism: these are the two sides of Davies' view of everything in the universe, including his own death. Novelist John Cowper Cowys called this philosophical approach the true Shakespearean attitude toward life. During our talk, Davies, polite and attentive, unveils learned and radical opinions about evil, God, Christianity, Gnosticism, compassion, Jung, science, and atheism. More than most people, he is open to all of these concepts — yet skeptical about each, too.

We start out talking about his deep interest in Christian Gnosticism, a movement based on the teachings of Jesus that was denounced as a heresy by orthodox church fathers in the second century. When I was arranging this session, I told Davies over the phone that I had acquired a copy of a McGill University Ph.D. thesis tracing the Gnostic spirit in Davies' novels. It was written by The Reverend Brian Thorpe, who went on to become executive secretary of the British Columbia Conference of the United Church.

Davies knew the thesis and thought it well done. But he suggests that Thorpe had gone too far; he would claim no expertise in Gnosticism.

Yet it turns out Davies' attraction to the movement went back for decades. "You see," he explains, his voice firm, but gentle with age, "the history of Gnosticism is all written by its enemies. And it's only just now that people are beginning to sift out what it may have really been about. And of course the church is very, very much down on it.

"I have a very unpopular theory of why that is. It's because the church worked on the theory that salvation is free; as long as you believed, you were saved. But the Gnostics thought you had to have some brains. The Gnostics taught that salvation, or enlightenment, could only be achieved through an inner journey." (*Gnosis* is Greek for "knowledge.") This, he continues, rules out great numbers of people with no intellectual equipment or spiritual muscle.

Davies knows his stand seemed elitist. But elitist is a label the Ontario-born novelist has learned to live with, in part because of his British accent and the buttoned-down decorum he retains from his days at Upper Canada College in Toronto and Balliol College, Oxford.

Davies also champions another concept from Gnosticism: a key role for *sophia*, which is the Greek word for wisdom, and represents a feminine metaphor for God.

"The church couldn't stand the idea of a goddess, because Christianity is strictly a monotheistic, male-oriented religion," he explains. "Christianity has had very remarkable effects, and has worked very well in certain ways, but I think the time has come when we've got to recognize there's a side of existence the Christian church has been shutting out for 2,000 years: half the human race."

Davies' fascination with Gnosticism and the feminine aspect of divinity dates back to his study of Jung at the age of thirty-five, long before the recent widespread burst of interest. In 1993, *sophia* became the controversial focus of the Reimagining Conference in Minneapolis, where 2,200 women from the world's mainstream churches gathered to "reimagine" Christianity in ways more sensitive to females. Some traditional Christians denounced the conference and the concept of *sophia* as pagan.

Although Davies isn't aware of this emerging and crucial theological debate over *sophia*, he feels that God plainly has a feminine side. "How could it be otherwise?" he asked incredulously. "It is such a crazy notion, when the whole generation and continuity of life relies on two sexes, to suppose that God manages on his own. But I have to be very, very careful what I say about this, because I could give terrible offence. So don't get me into a lot of trouble."

If Davies thinks God has a feminine aspect, can he define God?

He answers promptly, "No I can't. And I think that attempts to do so are often pretentious."

The problem with most definitions of God, according to Davies, is that they're not inclusive enough. When Davies was a boy in small-town Ontario, raised in a Presbyterian church by his conventionally religious parents, he had to memorize the Shorter Catechism. The second question of the Shorter Catechism is: "What is God?"

"And the answer is," he recites, "'God is the spirit, eternal, unchangeable in His goodness, mercy, and truth.'"

He finds it a superb definition, but "remarkably dry bread, isn't it? It's very Presbyterian, sort of a Puritanical description."

This reluctance to define God introduces a key aspect of his worldview: the willingness to accept mystery — to maintain tension between open-mindedness and gullibility, to humbly accept that humans won't ever understand everything.

Davies has always believed in God; in fact he feels it would be "shallow folly" not to do so. "I'm interested in atheists. They're like people who've cut off both hands," he said.

What does he mean?

"They've lost touch." For the first and only time in our talk, he explodes into a sharp, loud laugh at this joke. "They've lost touch with the whole universe."

When I suggest that a lot of atheists are decent people, he readily agrees. Moments before I talked to Davies, who was in Vancouver for the Writers' Festival, I saw him have a pleasant conversation with Mordecai Richler, a secular Jew who was treated harshly by his orthodox Jewish relatives and counts himself a determined atheist.

Nevertheless, Davies doesn't mince words over what he believes. "You see, a lot of atheism is not a matter of principle. It's just a matter of disillusion. And disillusion is romanticism. And romanticism is generally a negative force."

Nor does he hold back on his critique of agnosticism. John Irving is one of Davies' greatest admirers, a fellow appreciator of both credulity and skepticism. But Davies has little time for the agnostic position Irving ultimately takes. Most agnostics, says Davies, just don't want to be bothered fully exploring the spiritual possibilities they've rejected, "yet they try to make an intellectual position out of it."

Although Davies dares not try to define God, he does think people should try to be aware of "the numinous," the presence of the divine in everything. Churches haven't done enough of it. "Too many Christian churches focus on social work," he grumbles, "and too many religions behave as if humans are Lord of Creation and everything else is subject to them."

At the time of our talk, Davies was living in the rural Ontario town of Caledon, where he was constantly made aware of divinity as a perpetual aspect of animal and plant life. He once proposed native-Indian-style pantheism as something for us all to consider, but says now he did so mainly to irritate orthodox people. Told about an emerging concept in neo-classic Christian theology called *panentheism*, which teaches that God is both within everything and transcends everything, Davies says with a chuckle that it seems a very good principle to work on.

Although people should be aware of the numinous in all things, he warns that "you can't keep in touch with it all the time because you'd go mad."

He rapped his fingers on the table in front of him, its dark cherry hue reflecting the hotel salon's luxuriously dark, old-world decor. "What's that?" he asks.

I play along with the philosophical exercise by saying it appears to be a table, at least on the surface.

"Yes, I know," he says. "But if you start to look into what it really is, you'll probably end up being carried away somewhere." It's not necessarily humans' business to find out the true nature of a table, he continues. "Instead, it's our business to carry on our part, which is a much humbler one than we suppose, in the work of the universe. The notion that we are directing the universe, and setting it right, is an extraordinarily vain one."

He switches topics suddenly. "Now we're getting into something that will get you and me into a lot of trouble if we pursue it," he says, eyes dancing. "You see, if you consider this whole neo-Platonic idea of the universe, and consider the neo-Platonic notion of the succession of Zodiacal eons, we are just winding up the eon of Pisces."

My look must have shown I don't really understand what he is talking about.

He continues: "We are entering an age of flux. We are beginning to enter the eon of Aquarius."

Suddenly I get it: astrology.

I have read Davies' novels delving into magic, alchemy, dreams, mythology, and spiritual healing (this last was the subject of his last novel, *The Cunning Man*), but somehow I wasn't ready for astrology. His discussion of the ancient art of predicting events based on the position of heavenly bodies again shows his credulity, leavened with doubt.

"We are just winding up the eon of Pisces. The eon of Pisces is signified by two fish — one going one way and one going the other." He shapes his fingers, one of which carries a giant black ring, to symbolize fish moving in opposite directions: "This way is going toward persecution and war, and this way is going toward compassion and peace."

His voice picks up energy. He describes how we are seeing many signs now of flux — the Age of Aquarius. "We're getting into an age of bitter wars of brother against brother, like the business in the

Balkans. But what's happening? We're sending for the first time in human history things called 'peacekeeping teams.' And a lot of them come from this country. And that is a very remarkable development. And that is flux."

Anticipating my next question, he says, "These are ideas which are utterly discredited by all sensible thinkers. But ideas that are discredited by all prominent thinkers you should take a look at. There's something in it which they can't stand." He smiles. Why not? Davies' characters, after all, frequently pooh-pooh science and standard educational institutions for squashing imagination and wonder.

By astrology, Davies doesn't mean popular Horoscope columns, which predict whether a particular day is good for an individual to make an investment or get into a relationship. That's silly, he says, and much different from the astrology that Jung explored, which deals with world movements. "You mustn't shut out something like astrology, which extraordinarily clever people have believed in for centuries."

He readily acknowledges he has no real idea what the coming Zodiacal shift into the Age of Aquarius means. But he does believe that whatever is about to happen — whether peace or chaos — is inevitable. "I'm not a great believer in the idea that we control these things. I think they happen because of something not entirely in our grasp."

Despite Davies' sympathy for astrology and Gnosticism, he says he sometimes attends church, including St. James's Anglican Cathedral near the University of Toronto's Massey College, where he was master emeritus. It would be ridiculous, he asserts, to say he is not a Christian. He just didn't want to be typecast as one.

Davies feels Christianity has brought extraordinary things into the world. "One of them is compassion, which is enormously widespread in modern life. You see, when you consider the time when Christ was born, there was not, I suppose, a hospital anywhere in the world. And care of the poor was an entirely private and personal matter, and the rejection of anybody who was in some ways an outcast of society, a leper or something like that, was total and cruel. Christianity altered all that."

Although Davies tells me he believes in the power of compassion — and tries to guide his life by such basic values as decency and consideration for others — he insists that he doesn't actually try to do good. "You just create muddles that way." A strong desire to do good can be highly destructive, he said. "Consider the whole Christian missionary movement. Do you think that it did good in the world? It did a lot of damage. An excess of zeal to do good to others is bad stuff."

Davies denies that Jesus was lovey-dovey to everybody. "I think a lot of stories about him were just made up about him after his death, to sanitize him." He points out that Jesus balanced his love for people with righteous anger. "The man who cursed the fig tree and flogged the moneychangers out of the temple wasn't just eaten up with compassion."

The Jungian in Davies, he says, acknowledges the importance of recognizing the dark side of our personalities. "If you understand your dark side, or shadow side, you have to some extent defused it, because you recognize it when it's working. The point is any excess is bad. That is a very ancient Greek principle."

Given his willingness to support spiritual ideas far outside the mainstream, it is hard at first to see Davies as a man of moderation in all things. But he must have been doing something right to produce such a rich body of work and maintain a marriage for forty-eight years to Brenda, a former actress. She knits throughout our talk, saying at the end that she enjoyed it because it was far less predictable than most interviews.

It is late 1993, and Davies seems to be in brisk health. This didn't stop him, of course, from contemplating my final questions about death. He doesn't want to live forever, he says. "A lot of people take a rather narrow and unthinking notion of death. They want a kind of personal immortality. But would you want to go on being yourself forever? Anybody with enough brains to come in out of the rain would get sick of themselves. That foolishly neglected poet, Tennyson, put it marvelously. 'The life of a man who is fated to live forever is an absolute misery. He's sick of himself before he's 100 years old.'"

Davies says he had no idea what will happen after the Pale Horse arrives. "But I will tell you something to think about. What is it that makes a human being go? It is energy. And the physicists tell us that energy never vanishes. So when the body is worn out and dies, where does the energy go?"

Does he believe human consciousness survives death?

"You should never rule out any possibility. The scientists are always discovering something is possible they didn't think was possible before."

He admits that he fears death. But fear is not his last word on life's biggest mystery. He wonders what comes next. His final approach is one of openness. "Curiosity," he says, "is one of the great mainsprings of life."

The
Emerging Mystics

The new spirituality will be first and foremost an experience
of creative energy and inspiration.
— NICHOLAS BERDYAEV

Timothy Findley

NICK DIDLICK

"You get this overwhelming sense of how small you are in the Arctic. You can't ignore the fact you're only a part of a vast whole. And it wants you. It's not there for us. We're there for it."

To understand Timothy Findley's spirituality, we first have to get Sebastian out of the way. Well, not actually out of the way — perish the thought. For more than thirty-five years, the scruffy teddy bear has gone everywhere with Findley. It would be sacrilegious to shunt him aside. We just have to explain the significance of Sebastian, and how the crudely stitched *ursus carnivora* serves as a rock of ages for Findley, one of Canada's most acclaimed novelists.

Once, while hiking a treacherous mountain pass, Findley's guide told everyone to throw out all nonessentials. Findley threw away his boots, but kept Sebastian. Sebastian goes everywhere. "I guess it's superstition, to a degree," he admits. Yet if he were away from his farm near Stone Orchard, Ontario, and unpacked his bag and discovered Sebastian wasn't there, he says he wouldn't leave his hotel. "I'd be petrified what it would mean — the plane would crash or whatever."

Then he laughs. We shouldn't get too deeply serious about this worn, stuffed animal, he says, his eyes liquid under thick gray hair as he gazes at Sebastian on the table beside him. If Sebastian disappeared, he admits he'd be worried, but mostly in a distracted way. "I've invested him with meaning; you invest all kinds of objects with meaning. And most of it is pleasurable. It's for the fun of looking at him at home, and being able to say, 'This body has been everywhere that this body has been.'"

Findley doesn't have the heart to take Sebastian with him in death, however. He's dropped his plan to cremate Sebastian when his own corpse goes up in smoke. "I can't do that to him," he chortles. "Isn't that crazy?" He considers giving his cuddly talisman away as part of his archives, so Sebastian can have some meaning for someone else.

Beyond Sebastian, Findley, the author of *The Piano Man's Daughter* and *Headhunter*, as well as the award-winning *The Telling of Lies* and *Famous Last Words*, harbors a more challenging spirituality. Like many writers and artists, he finds spirituality in nature, specifically in the Arctic, which he visited long ago.

His early years with the church, in his case the United Church of Canada, are ridden with scars, as they are for so many North Americans of his generation. Findley is only now finding a level of rapprochement.

Where to begin his critique of religion? Chronologically, it would start several thousand years ago, when monotheism took hold. The world, says Findley, has never recovered from humanity's decision to accept only one God. "In that moment, we turned away from the holiness of everything that is. Prior to that point, every rock, every drop of water, every beast, every person, every thing, was holy."

Findley explored the roots of monotheism in his spectacularly imaginative book *Not Wanted on the Voyage*, in which he portrayed Noah as an authoritarian patriarch creating God in an image that would benefit males. To find Findley's next enemy of faith, we jump forward to the apostle Paul. "I shouldn't say it," he says, but does anyway: "Paul should be lined up against a wall, with a number of others, and shot. What he did to Christianity was vile." Findley thinks Paul was "the first manipulator" of Christianity, who twisted Jesus' words to make the religion a list of "shall nots." Paul, he says, is the source of all the troubles that women and gays have had with the church.

Zooming forward to the 1950s and his teen years, Findley lashes out at how church ministers used Paul's antihomosexual views to reject him. "I'm afraid I got put off the church and its mythology because of the church's attitude to my sexual orientation. I would say things to them in great anger, or sometimes in tears: 'You bastards! How can you call yourselves Christians?'"

For similar reasons, Findley grows incredulous as he moves on to Pope John Paul II. "Here we are living in the age of AIDS and the age of terrible starvation and ghastly poverty and the Pope is still out there saying, 'No birth control. No abortion. No condoms.' To me, it's grotesquely immoral. It's like someone walking out and saying, 'I am the Vicar of Christ and I want you all to die!' Well, thanks a bunch."

Findley stares out the Vancouver hotel window early in our talk, making little eye contact, holding his glasses with his refined fingers. But as he picks up momentum, his words pour like water. Findley's long-time partner, Bill Whitehead, told me beforehand that Findley was looking forward to talking about religion; he certainly seems to be reveling in it. Sebastian appears to listen intently.

On the topic of world affairs, Findley displays his social ethics, which are not for the squeamish. These views inform his dark, futuristic vision in *Headhunter*, in which North America is ruled by the rich solely for the rich. Findley worries that most governments today rule for corporations, not people. So he hates the free trade deals among the United States, Canada, and Mexico. "We're on a free ride on NAFTA all the way to hell," he says. Findley is famous for his red-hot views of politicians who sell out to big money.

But even as he boils over about free trade, a glint of delight flickers in his eyes. He knows he's ranting. On one level he enjoys the chance to air his provocative opinions.

There is more than rage behind Findley's spiritual, ethical worldview. There is also a wellspring of hope, conviction, and respect for human dignity. As a kid, Findley remembers his grandmother conducting Easter vigils on her knees. "I was very respectful of her. She would watch with Jesus through the night and that was a great hardship for an old woman. That was her devotion to the mythology, which is what I think makes that stuff work."

He also deeply appreciates a request from Toronto's Bloor Street United Church in 1980 to read from the pulpit on a Sunday. "My God, it was incredible," he enthuses. He picked a passage from *The Wars* where Mrs. Ross storms out of church after the preacher urges young men to fight and die in the First World War. "Mrs. Ross," he explains, "was not buying into all this patriotic nonsense, which basically says, 'Kill all our children.' When the preacher talked about the need for war, she stomped out and sat in the snow. It was hair-raising. And then a young girl comes and stares at her. They have a conversation. And Mrs. Ross realizes, 'I've frightened this child by sitting here in the snow. And I have a responsibility.' And she asks the child to go with her in to the church and when they walk in the choir is singing 'Praise God from Whom All Blessings Flow.' And there's a kind of reconciliation. She is never reconciled to Christianity's part in the war, but she is reconciled to the fact her spiritual self cannot turn its back on the best of what is there to be had."

As Findley finished reading the passage, the choir at Bloor Street United began singing "Praise God from Whom All Blessings Flow." "Wow," he recalls. "I tell you, I had to look the other way."

After the service, he went upstairs with the Reverend Lois Wilson, a former moderator of the United Church of Canada and president of the World Council of Churches. He also talked to Dr. Robert MacLure, another prominent United Church leader whom Findley considers a wonderful man. Leaning forward, Findley says, "We sat down just as we are sitting now, and he thumped me on the knee with his hand and he said, 'Do you realize your grandfather, Findley, was my Sunday school teacher?' And he said, 'I used to delight in throwing spitballs at your dad and he did not know where they were coming from.' So old MacLure was a rascal. I felt a sense of reconciliation — for their generosity in having offered this venue for me to tell this story about how someone lost their faith. I think it was an extraordinary gesture."

In 1988, the United Church of Canada, the country's largest Protestant denomination with 800,000 members, became one of the first major Christian groups on the continent to allow the ordination of gays who are in active relationships. It was about time, of course, in Findley's opinion. If the church had shown such boldness when he was young, things might have been different.

Many of Findley's spiritual beliefs are not too far from what some Christians think. He is drawn, for example, to what he calls the harshness of Jesus. "He cut through all the bullshit. That's the whole meaning of the episode in the temple; that's the whole meaning of the forty days in the desert; that's the whole meaning of the Garden of Gethsemane. The guy was real, and we've turned him into a sentimental twit."

But while he admires Jesus' teaching, Findley discovered the sacred outside the church, in the summer of 1969 while camping with Whitehead on the endless tundra of the Northwest Territories. Findley was awestruck by the stark, ethereal vastness of the Arctic. As the desert inspired so many mystics of long ago, the largely unspoiled Canadian Arctic now seems to possess the power to transform people spiritually.

"You get this overwhelming sense of how small you are in the Arctic. You can't ignore the fact you're only a part of a vast whole. And it wants you. It's not there for us. We're there for it. That was the epiphany for me. I came to understand up there my place in the scheme of things. It was a wonderful breakthrough to realize the spirit is out there in everything — in the trees themselves, in all the hardship and all the wonders."

Findley refuses to confine this spirit to a doctrine. Some current philosophers and theologians, however, might describe Findley's epiphany as an example of God's incarnation in all things. The new technical word for this idea is *panentheism* — a term used by process philosophers such as Charles Hartshorne and creation theologians such as Matthew Fox to oppose *theism*, which teaches that we are here and God is out there somewhere. Many traditional Christians, Jews, and Muslims are theists who imagine God as a distant ruler supernaturally imposing things from without.

Panentheism is also to be distinguished from *pantheism*, which assumes that everything *is* God. Many New Age believers are pantheists. Pantheism denies that God transcends nature, while panentheism posits that God is *in* all things and all things are *in* God. Or in

Findley's words, "the spirit is out there in everything."

Findley is an artist, however, not a philosopher. He hesitates to reduce anything to a formula, including life after death, a concept that is much in his mind these days. In his memoir *Inside Memory*, he writes: "Be grateful, in your final hour, for life. Not for you life alone, but for the fact of life: for everything that is. After all is said and done, I know I will have no answers. None. I don't expect to have them. What I will have, and all I have now, is questions. What I have done — what I have tried to do — is frame those questions — not with question marks — but in the paragraphs of books. . . . I am still, and will always be, myself alone. But, as myself, I know, now, I am not alone."

My impression from spending time with Findley is he has found more answers than *Inside Memory* reveals. Now in his mid-sixties, with his parents, grandparents, cousins, and many friends now dead, some from AIDS, Findley doesn't fear death. He just finds life too wonderful to give up easily. Sometimes, he says, gazing at the stars, he feels the affirming presence of those he cared about. "They loved the fields. They loved the animals. They loved one another. They loved it all. And I can't just say, 'Well, they're gone now.'"

He is silent for a long time. "They're not gone. They've got to be out there somewhere, in whatever form. This is why it's so important to come to the place where we actually do regard everything as holy, where we invest the world with spirit."

He has difficulty articulating this conviction, he says — a big admission for a writer. "I don't believe in heaven. And I don't believe in getting up and looking at my watch and thinking, 'Well, that was an interesting little time spent down on that planet. And now I'm somewhere else.' I can't grasp that. But I do think there are spiritual residues — the spiritual aspect of who they are is there. And it's there in time as well."

His complex, mystical convictions are tumbling out now. "I think of time as a continuum. I don't think time is ever over. I think it's all there behind us. If one could walk backwards in time, all these people would be there. That's how we live our hour. You and I are having this moment. When we get up and walk away, it's passed into time. It's not gone."

This moment, those loved ones, will never be lost. Everything is holy. Sebastian seems to agree.

Peter C. Newman

NICK DIDICK

*"The idea is not merely to believe in spiritual intuitions,
but to rely on them."*

When he was young, Peter Newman had no time for religion. With the
Nazi party on the rise, it was dangerous to be a Jew in Czechoslovakia.
At age ten, he and his wealthy parents were forced to dodge tanks and
machine-gun bursts as they escaped Nazi forces. "Being Jewish was not
a very comfortable faith because you gave your life to it. My youth was
spent in running away. We did not have a sense of continuity and community and worship. I was just lucky to be alive."

Newman, whose books on history, politics, and the economic establishment have sold more than two million copies, has a subtle air of sadness and discontent, not surprising perhaps in a man who has suffered a mobile childhood, a harsh (though self-imposed) work life, and three marriage breakups.

At the time of our interview in 1993, signs of his worldly success are front and center. He lives in a spectacular, cliff-hugging, waterfront home in North Vancouver's Deep Cove, thirty minutes from downtown Vancouver. His rich, green leather furniture is arranged precisely, and a side room is filled with perfectly ordered filing cabinets. His giant desk looks out onto yachts tied up in a marina and shorebirds on a rocky, calm beach.

Newman boasts a resume many writers would sell a child for. He has written fifteen books about politics, history, and business, including *The Canadian Establishment*, *The Acquisitors*, *The Bronfman Dynasty*, and *The Company of Adventurers*. He has made the *New York Times* bestseller lists more than once. He has been chief editor at Canada's leading newsmagazine, *Maclean's*, and Canada's biggest paper, the *Toronto Star*. It would take too much space to list his awards and honorary degrees.

He is bashful talking about spiritual issues, although he says that lately, in his sixties, he is beginning to explore ways to access the spirit. His conversation veers back and forth between eloquent statements and tentative, half-finished sentences. A few months later, he acknowledges that our talk was a significant factor in nudging him further along a spiritual path.

Although Newman's grandparents were devout Jews, and he has read a great deal about the Judeo-Christian tradition, he has only been to synagogue twice, once for a wedding and once to give a speech. The Holocaust crushed any chances of orthodox faith for him. "I found it very difficult to understand if there was a God, why he allowed six million Jews to be slaughtered who were totally innocent, including both sets of my grandparents who died in concentration camps. It shakes the reawakening of a faith. All of a sudden, somebody decided all these people had to die. It's ridiculous."

It is not, he admits, a rational reason for unbelief. Newman is working out his own answer to what theologians call *theodicy*, the question "If God is all-good and all-powerful, why do terrible things happen?"

His voice drops to a hush as he reveals what he does believe. "I believe in a Supreme Being, a creator of the universe, someone who nurtures the universe — but not a just healer. I believe there is a Supreme Being who has his or her faults." When I say he sounds like a Jewish prophet, daring to criticize the Supreme Being, he laughs. But he is not being facetious.

He reads a quote from philosopher George Santayana that helps him explain his emerging mystical point of view: "The world is not respectable; it is mortal, confused, tormented, deluded forever. But it is also shot through with beauty, with love, with glints of courage and laughter. In these, the spirit looms timidly and struggles to the light amid the thorns."

Many answers have been posed to the problem of why evil exists. Some claim that God inflicts suffering on us to teach us lessons. Others suggest the Supreme Being allows us the illusion of freedom so that we can learn to be responsible. The assumption is that such an all-powerful God could take that freedom away at any point and manipulate the desired result.

I tell Newman I'm impressed by a version of theodicy described by American process theologian David Ray Griffin in *The Problem of Evil*. Griffin and others suggest that the answer to the puzzle of evil is to alter one part of the formula. God is, indeed, all-loving, but *not* all-powerful. God's power is persuasive, not coercive. God offers us a loving possibility in each moment, but humans have real freedom to choose to respond or not. Humans have the terrifying freedom to fail catastrophically; witness the Holocaust. This fragile view of human destiny is less comforting to some. But it is perhaps more realistic than the standard theological solutions. Newman acknowledges that the idea makes sense.

Whatever glimmers of spiritual contentment he has achieved, says Newman, have come from outside organized religion — literally outside, while sailing on his thirty-five-foot sloop, *Indra.* "When I go sailing, I visit the peaceable kingdom, especially here."

He gazes out the window of his immaculate office-cum-living room, at the imposing, snow-crusted mountains shooting up out of the waters of Indian Arm, a long inlet with steep cliffs. "These waters are a holy place." Sailing brings release, he explains, from what Cervantes called "the melancholy burden of sanity."

When he's working, Newman leads a stressful, solitary life. He spends up to sixteen hours at a computer at his desk under the high ceiling of his nautical-themed house, with its starboard-green and port-red lights at the front door. "To be a writer is to meet deadlines," he sighs. "Your mind gets burnt out." He produces numerous magazine columns each month while continuing to work on books. Like many people today, Newman is weary, and concerned: "There's so much going out, nothing coming in."

Sailing gives him something back. Whether on a trip to the Queen Charlotte Islands or around Vancouver's harbor, he is far away from deadlines and the city, in touch with the sea and its creatures under the vast sky of the Pacific. "To me the most touching experience of all is when you suddenly encounter a pod of killer whales. I turn off the engine and just drift through the pod. It's such a supreme experience.

Once when this happened, for about an hour later all of us on the sailboat just whispered." He explains the attraction of sailing with a line from Joseph Conrad, who defined sailors as "the grown-up children of a discontented earth."

By the time Newman ties up again in port, he sees the world in a different way. "The day kind of folds into itself. The crew are hugging themselves against the chill of the evening. You tie the boat up and you're back to earth. Whether it's a day sail or a long trip, you return with a heightened sensitivity to everything around you. You see the world anew, freshly and vividly. There's a surge of inner excitement that the best of urban experiences can never match. You enter another dimension. And that's not just a way of talking. It's very real."

Although being outside can be a mystical event for Newman, he doesn't find God in the wind and water. "I don't use the word 'God.' I wouldn't say 'God' because then people would think you're talking about a guy with a white beard. Just as a footnote to nothing, I've always wondered whether God looked like Robertson Davies, or Robertson Davies looked like God," he says, smiling. "You certainly get a feeling of a great spiritual being when you're out there on the water. But 'God' is too limiting; it becomes a Catholic God or a Presbyterian God or it becomes too precise an image for people. And I don't have that precise image. It's more a pervasive mood than a guy with a white beard."

Newman finds this "pervasive mood," or feeling, not only on the sea, but in music, which he listens to while writing. With one of his hundred Stan Kenton jazz CDs playing on four giant speakers in his acoustically designed living room/office, he'll sometimes stop typing to "conduct" with a baton. "I know all the scores. It's a way of getting into the music, instead of being an inactive listener. It gives me the cadence for my writing and it gives me energy."

When he combines sailing and music, Newman finds the experience sublime. With his sailboat's exterior waterproof speakers bouncing his favorite scores off the West Coast mountains, he says, "the whole world becomes my cathedral."

Sailing a stormy sea or rough passage represents for Newman another theme of his life: challenge. "Sailing can be a proving ground for the soul," he says. "A true existentialist sets himself goals and tries to meet them. He may not do it, but if he doesn't try, he diminishes himself. It's important to come up with challenges in your life, to come up with some meaningful crusades."

Newman himself crusades to preserve the values of Canada, the country that took him and his Jewish refugee family in when no others would. He founded the Committee for an Independent Canada, as well as the Friends of Public Broadcasting, and has campaigned against free trade with the United States and Mexico. "I've never taken this country for granted. I've always defended us from Americans and whoever wants to distort our values. I'm not anti-American, but I want us to live according to our values, not imported values." Free trade, he says, has handed the U.S. giant a wedge to loosen the independence of Canadian government, business, and culture.

"It is absolutely weakening the authority of government. The Canadian business establishment was totally behind free trade, but it is also weakened by it. The Canadian establishment was not holy, but at least it was our own. Now we're ruled by a foreign establishment. In the European Economic Community, the countries can operate as equals. But we have no clout against the United States, where the only value is competition. Free trade has mortally wounded the east-west connections that hold this country together, which we've had to pay for. Public cultural institutions such as the CBC have been invaluable in keeping this country together. So I work hard for these causes."

The Canadian values he fights to preserve include gentleness, a commitment to peace, order and good government, respect for an honest day's work, and a willingness to compromise. He calls the last of these "a secular commandment on how to live our life." These principles, he says, may sound dull compared to the Americans' "life, liberty, and the pursuit of happiness," but they have produced a caring, humane, civil nation.

The value Newman cherishes most, however, has for him been the most elusive: love.

After three marriages, he still believes relationships are crucial. "The only two things that matter in life are love and faith," he says. The words came out slowly, tenderly, with a scent of sadness. "Since I don't have a hell of a lot of faith, I'm still searching for love. It's a central part of my life. I think you reach a plateau of spiritual contentment through love — and only through love."

A few months after our first talk, I meet Newman again at a banquet and he tells me he has been smitten by a woman who practises spiritual healing. He is beginning a serious exploration of alternative forms of spirituality — what some would call New Age religion.

Two years later, he agrees to another interview. It is now 1995, and he is putting his considerable energy into a new crusade: integrating spiritual values into business. Teaming up with corporate partners such as B.C. Hydro, Westcoast Energy, and the giant VanCity Credit Union, he organized a major international conference called "The New Spirit of Work: Empowerment in Business."

I visit him in a small Kitsilano apartment that looks out on freighters in the distance in English Bay. With its worn furniture, it is a modest, functional place compared to the Deep Cove mansion, which he has sold, partly because it was too isolated from friends in Vancouver. He is staying in this apartment until he finishes his latest book, *The Canadian Revolution: From Deference to Defiance.* Newspapers and books are piled knee-high on the floor as he serves an informal lunch of jellied consommé and make-your-own sandwiches on a small coffee table.

"Spiritual strength among employees will be invaluable if businesses hope to become competitive, productive, and happy places," he says. Standard full-time jobs and traditional corporate culture are disappearing. "People who work will need to find spiritual resources within themselves if they and their businesses are to prosper. Workers will have to find contentment in themselves, rather than simply buying into a corporate race."

The tentativeness of our first interview has evaporated, replaced with a refined but clear spiritual vision of work and life. Newman's emerging spirituality is not based on belief in an all-powerful, Almighty God. Instead, he defines spirituality as "a way of personal empowerment, of being in touch with your feelings, of being totally honest and knowing there's some Supreme Being to commune with, who is not a big guy with a cloak and beard."

He has also come out of the spiritual closet, mounting a partial defence of New Age spirituality in his business column in *Maclean's* — a tough spot from which to stand up for a notion that is decidedly unfashionable in most parts. The column stressed how the New Age movement is about transcending established religious dogma and stressing the spiritual instead of the materialistic. It also praises British Columbia, where Newman moved in the early 1980s to escape the relentless pace of Toronto. He gives me a copy of the column.

"[The New Age movement] requires being so open to new experiences that instead of planning the detailed path of one's life, one allows it to unfold. The idea is not merely to believe in spiritual intuitions but to rely on them . . . . Spirituality cannot be achieved by life in the fast lane . . . . It is concerned more with listening and learning than with preaching or competing."

Newman predicted that many of his Eastern friends and contacts would think that including such vulnerable, passionate thoughts in his column, and indeed his whole pursuit of a spiritual life, was crazy. They did.

"Who cares?" he says. He's not about to look back. Staring out over the bay where his beloved sailboat is tied up, he grabs another can of ginger beer from the fridge and says, "I don't know how pursuing a more spiritual life is going to work out in the end, but it would be absurd not to try."

Robert Bly

"In ritual space, the competition disappears."

Toward the end of an evening of storytelling, philosophizing, and bazouki playing, a thirty-something man asks Robert Bly if he truly believes, as he had suggested, that a man must first face his own father before he can love a woman.

"I don't know," the undisputed leader of the mytho-poetic men's movement replies before more than a thousand affection-filled listeners. "It may be true. It may not. Don't depend on me."

The unpredictability of a poet. After the laughs die out from the sold-out, three-quarters-male audience at the University of British Columbia on this Saturday night, the mentor to millions of North American men tries to sidestep the pressure to be a guru. "Grieving" over a rotten relationship with his angry, alcoholic father proved to be the door that opened up Bly's understanding of manhood and male-female relations, but he tells his audience (a couple of whom he hugged at intermission) that they must find their own door.

The next morning, gulls over the beach of English Bay are squealing in the mist outside a top room in the old Sylvia Hotel. In his late sixties, Bly growls a little tune as he dons his trademark vest, which, together with his bird's-nest of white hair, his irreverent humor, and his gift of the gab, rounds out the impression of a modern Mark Twain — but without the cynicism. His wife, Ruth, who often leads workshops with Bly, grabs an umbrella and goes for a walk in the rain with a Vancouver acquaintance.

The mytho-poetic men's movement, which is indirectly based on the work of the late mythologist Joseph Campbell, who taught that the legends and stories of ancient cultures can teach us how to live today, has touched a lot of men in recent years, largely on the strength of this Minnesota-born poet's gruff charm and incisive blend of psychology and spirituality. Bly has written many little-known poetry books, including the U.S. National Book Award-winning *Light Around the Body*. But *Iron John*, Bly's complex, mythological prose novel about a boy's initiation into manhood, rose for about a year to the top of best-seller lists in the early nineties. And Bill Moyers's profile of Bly, *A Gathering of Men*, replays again and again on TV. Since the early 1980s, the workshops Bly gives all around North America with Ruth, with other storytellers, or with Jungian psychologist Marion Woodman of Toronto, sell out months in advance. With his 1996 book,

Sibling Culture, about how men need to be fathers to their children, not friends, Bly is again pushing men to discover what it means to be a modern, authentic male.

Bly has become famous for encouraging men to rediscover their inner "warrior" through initiation rites, wilderness retreats, and male mentors. But he's not talking about war-makers. He was disgusted by the American attempt to "heal" the wounds of Vietnam by attacking Iraq, for example. President George Bush needed wise older men to initiate him into real manhood. Bush, he says, flip-flopped between the two usual male extremes: macho and wimp.

Bly's thesis is that the Industrial Revolution separated sons from fathers, for the first time forcing men to work away from home to earn a living. Boys now receive not teaching from their fathers, but the brunt of their "irritable after-work temperament."

Bly's journey into mytho-poetic men's work began after he and Ruth, who live together in a log cabin in Minnesota, brought up three daughters without much trouble — "it seemed to go sweetly" — but then discovered raising their younger two children, both sons, was much more difficult. "I felt there was going to be a problem. It's a father's job to know what he wants to pass on to his boys from the male line of his family. I suddenly didn't know what I wanted to pass on. And I knew if I didn't decide, I'd pass on everything — including the brutality, the distance, the alcoholism. I had to ask myself, 'What does it mean to have a son?' Was I going to be a channel for all my father's habits or was I going to be a teacher, a mentor?"

He's a pleasant challenge to interview, being both fervent and approachable. Ask a question, and you never know what you might get in return — a blunt dismissal or a lengthy confabulation. When asked how he understands God, he delivers both.

First he says curtly, "You have to deduce that from what I say."

Then, slowly, his thoughts begin to emerge, like a great bear from a den. He has reflected long and hard about religious traditions and how people can find strength through them. "Joe Campbell would say even using words like God is a mistake. He would talk about being 'transparent to the transcendent' — that 'something,' far beyond the human, that cannot be described in human terms. The important thing is not to talk about it, certainly not to praise it, but to be transparent to it. The point is to arrange the molecules in your body so some of its radiant darkness comes through."

He refuses to try to define divinity any further. Instead, Bly aims to revive "ritual space." Although he credits the Christian Church with preserving mythology for a couple of millennia, and not allowing the Romans "to turn the entire globe into a shopping mall," he believes Protestantism, and, increasingly, modern Catholicism, is ignorant of ritual space. Psychology also fails. "Psychological discussion of men's lives is helpful, but in the end, not very meaningful, because psychology doesn't understand about ritual space. That's a very harsh and lopsided statement. But I like it."

He smiles with Twain-like cheekiness. Then he launches into explaining the spiritual roots of the mytho-poetic men's movement, which, he cautions, should not be confused with the other six men's movements: gay, black, traditional family, male rights, Marxist, and pro-feminist.

"The best moment in the men's movement is when we're together in the woods for six days. It's not a bunch of wild men out there beating on drums and being savage. The woods merely isolate men from their Protestantism. They're able to remember some of the old memories of ritual space. In business, men don't really have companionship because of competition. But in ritual space, the competition disappears. The depth of feeling and eloquence that comes out is amazing."

I ask what he meant when he once referred to the men's movement as religious. "When you talk of myth and fairy tale, you immediately move into the area of the divine. And so it's religious in exactly the same way as when you walk into a church and you've been a stock-broker or something and suddenly you see a fantastic angel statue. And there's the Virgin Mary. You're in another world. You're talking about things not mentioned in other places. So that's why I say the men's movement, in the end, is a religious movement."

He has a lot of problems with organized Christianity, but is not about to write it off. The church, he says, has largely ignored ancient means of opening up to sacred reality: music, dance, and chanting. "The Protestants say, 'We don't want any of this. Please give us a boring sermon. The more boring it is, the more inadequate we'll feel.' That's what we associate with religion: being inadequate." Nevertheless, Bly respects the way the churches have kept alive some sense of spirituality through the centuries. "In the middle ages, the churches were the biggest buildings in the town. You knew the spirit was the most important thing in the culture. But now the bank towers are the biggest buildings. And business is the most important thing in this culture. Therefore the question is, 'How does the human being in this culture achieve any type of depth?'"

The last thing Bly wants to be is "tribalistic" about where depth, meaning, and divinity lie. He rejects the idea that divinity can reside in one religious figure such as Jesus. "Joseph Campbell said global wars would only end when we stop defining our gods as real and other peoples' gods as not real." While he sees much of the inner "warrior" in Jesus, he sees it as well in Buddha, and in Dionysus, the Greek god of ecstasy. Jesus was truly "obnoxious" when he overturned the money-changers' tables in the temple, Bly says, his voice rising, then falling to a near-mumble.

"Jesus was not a nice boy. He is not associated, in my mind, with being gentle and turning the other cheek. A way to madden a person completely is to say, after they slap you on the cheek, 'You haven't hit the other one yet.' You have to make a distinction between fierceness and brutality. Fierceness is the readiness to be fierce if you need to be . . . the inner warrior is the one who protects you from being shamed by others."

He pauses, then hums a bit, when asked about Buddha. "I don't know. Buddha is not as important to me as Jesus. But there's no question that Jesus is a supreme example of someone who is transparent to the divine." Was Buddha a warrior? "Absolutely. Joe Campbell used to tell the story of Buddha sitting under the trees and all the powers of death and fear and terror arrived. And all he did was reach down and touch the earth with one finger. What a great warrior."

After asking if I'd like a morning coffee, he puts the kettle on. The best thing he did for his boys, now in their twenties, he says, was to take them at age ten or eleven to a men's group to "sit around and laugh and drum and play music for a couple of hours. The boys' eyes get big and they realize their father is a part of something larger than their family." Most men, he asserts, have never passed through the Oedipal stage. "They're still attached to their mother and resentful of the father. We're in a desperate situation. Boys are rejecting older men, and throwing themselves on the mercy of women. They're making the women their mothers. So women are complaining, 'Where are the men out there? I see a lot of boys.'"

The last thing Bly wants to do is criticize women or feminism. He wants macho men to stop hating women, and "soft" men to stop imitating them. Nevertheless, Bly believes some women fear men gathering in groups. "To some extent, there's justified fear. A lot of men together is called a war. And in western culture the church has excluded women. It's outrageous women are not brought in by the Catholic Church," he says angrily. "So women don't want to be excluded from the religious, or mythic, side of men's work. But I think women have to realize the church is an institution and the men's movement is the beginning of vulnerability. Men say certain things to each other when women are not present. And that is not a criticism of women. Men and women shame each other so easily. So in the end, the more men are able to talk to each other without being shamed, the better husbands they will be."

The last question of the UBC evening was essentially religious: How does one remain hopeful?

Sitting on the hotel couch, looking rumpled, Bly agrees it was a wonderful question. The worst problem that afflicts North American culture, which is flooded with vacuous TV, movies, and music, is the lack of hope people feel because they cannot find meaning, he says.

"When ritual disappears and progress turns out to be not working, then people are starved for meaning. The greatest disease of contemporary times is the inability to find meaning. You can feel it after you watch television for an hour. Your body feels extremely upset because it has spent a whole hour and it hasn't taken in any meaning. So where do you find meaning? It's not going to be on the tube or in popular entertainment or in love stories. It's in great psychology and mythology and the stories of the ancestors. I also think there's hope in a life that has been lived." He pauses, listening to a click at the door.

Ruth comes in from her walk and puts the umbrella away. Bly remembers the kettle he put on to boil thirty minutes ago. "Oh, hell. You idiot!" he barks at himself. I tell him not to worry about coffee and he turns off the kettle. I get the impression he likes to be taken seriously, but not too seriously; he's not afraid of appearing human. As he tries to remember what he was talking about, he tells Ruth about the question about hope. She had noted it too.

"I know for the people who come to events like last night that they don't want to be taught by thirty-year-olds," Bly says. "They don't want to be taught by forty-year-olds. They'll reluctantly be taught by fifty-year-olds. But they'd rather have sixty-year-olds. Men want some meaning from older people who have thought over their lives. The young men want to know they can get to sixty and still feel a joy in life and a curiosity about what it could mean. They want to know you can be sixty and not be defeated."

Robert Fulghum

CRAIG HODGE

"I would like to end up sitting on the end of my grave and saying, 'Well, I didn't win the Nobel Prize, and I didn't win the Pulitzer Prize, but I won the Refrigerator Award.'"

Like the legendary Texan he is, this laid-back phenomenon does everything in a big way. Robert Fulghum's childlike musings have transformed him from a lower-middle-class Unitarian minister into one of the world's most financially successful authors. He's made more than $10 million from the book *All I Really Need to Know I Learned in Kindergarten.* Derided by some intellectuals, but loved by many thirsting for hope and meaning in a despairing world, Fulghum's little book has encircled the globe, selling nine million copies. Published in more than twenty-five languages, it topped the *New York Times* best-seller list forever.

Clothed in overalls, he settles his large body into an old wooden wheelchair near a woodstove in his gargantuan Seattle waterfront "studio" — actually a converted warehouse he's turned into an artistic playpen about the size of a football field. It has a kitchen, a dance floor, an office where staff handle mail and his charitable foundation, a room in which he and others create artwork, and a couch for his naps. His voice is rich and relaxed. His hair and beard are silver. Out comes a pipe.

Although Fulghum's entire philosophy is based on doing rather than talking, he's awfully adept at talking. While attending Star King Unitarian seminary in California, Fulghum became keenly conscious of what he personally believed. All students there were required each year to write a personal credo, defending its coherence against all comers. "It was tough," he admits. Since that time, he has streamlined his credo more each year, until now it has been boiled down to: "Your credo is what you do."

He says he has given away more than half the money he made from *Kindergarten* and follow-up books, including *Uh Oh: Some Observations from Both Sides of the Refrigerator Door.* He hands over a hundred thousand dollars here, fifty thousand there. . . . It's still flowing out. He doesn't think of this generosity as a big deal. It's certainly less trouble for him to give now than when he and his wife and four kids (now in their thirties) were scraping by and he was donating $25 at a time. "I don't want to go around saying, 'Hey, look at me!' Because I don't think I'm doing anything any different than I did when I was giving $25. In fact, it costs me less. It is less of an economic impact on me to write a big check now than it was to write a small check then. But I can't tell you how much joy it is to find out an organization is in trouble and write them a check for $100,000." Planned Parenthood, human rights organizations, the Salvation Army ("they're do folks, not talk folks"), the American Civil Liberties Union, Greenpeace, traditional Christian churches, and public radio and television are among those who have benefited from Fulghum's major donations.

Based on his public persona alone, it would be tempting to dismiss Fulghum, who is still technically a minister in the Unitarian Church, as a lightweight. "Most of what I really need to know about how to live and what to do and how to be, I learned in kindergarten," he wrote in his famous mini-essay, now also a popular poster, that formed the heart of *Kindergarten*. "Share everything. Play fair. Don't hit people," it begins. "Clean up your own mess . . . Say you're sorry when you hurt somebody. Flush. Warm cookies and cold milk are good for you . . . When you go out into the world, watch out for traffic, hold hands, and stick together. Be aware of wonder."

Yet during an afternoon spent running around Seattle with Fulghum to a bookstore and a grocery store, I discover much more in him than cuteness. Fulghum is easy to be with, but he has content. "People have misunderstood the point of the whole kindergarten thing," he says. "Its message is not that six-year-olds understand everything there is to know. It's that kindergarten introduces us to the most profound issues of existence. It's where individual ego first clashes with group needs. It's where the 'social contract' is hammered out."

The musings in *Kindergarten*, which he first told to Northwest United States Unitarian congregations of about 200 people each, are about how, when we're thrust into a world of strangers, we're not allowed to hit them, he says. "We're told to clean up our own damn mess." What could be a more important ecological lesson?

Kindergarten rules are as tough to live up to, he says, as the wisdom in Jesus' deceptively straightforward story about the Good Samaritan, an outcast who helps a man in trouble. "When the Samaritan was asked why he helped the man, he answered, 'Who is my neighbor?' I think that is one of the most challenging, difficult, awesome statements that has ever been made in Western religion. You could give a two-hour lecture on semantics, linguistics, theology, and philosophy, but you can't do much better than that. The story of the Good Samaritan is an action story. It asks, 'What are you going to do?'" He laughs heartily.

While he has little time for Mormon theology or Catholic dogma (which he calls some of "the different metaphors people form their lives by"), he says that doesn't stop him from often being impressed by the ethics of Mormons and Catholics. "I know people whose verbalization agrees 100 percent with mine, but whose action I can't endorse. And I know people whose metaphors are 180 degrees opposed to mine, but whose lives I fully sympathize with. As I get older, my words get shorter and my sense of acting gets larger."

Now entering his sixties, he still has a lot of child in him. But he also has a good chunk of adult. He has always known how to make things happen. About twenty-five years ago, when Fulghum was a regional superintendent for the Unitarian Church, Vancouverite Peggy Woods remembers how, without official approval, he put up $1,000 of his own money to hold a sixty-one-acre chunk of Kootenay forest in southwestern British Columbia so that it could some day become a retreat center. Now the Unitarian property is worth more than $1 million. "He's willing to take a risk," says Woods. "If he believes in something, he goes for it."

Fulghum doesn't know exactly where he got his damn-the-torpedoes worldview. As soon as he could, he left behind the strict, fundamentalist Southern Baptist upbringing of his Texan parents and headed for a northern U.S. college. "I was raised in Waco, Texas, which is pretty well considered the Vatican of the Southern Baptist Church because of Baylor University there. It was very fundamentalist, very conservative. My parents, my mother especially, were very active in the church and the church was very powerful in the community. It was a dry town. You couldn't even buy beer. In some ways it was a Southern version of Norman Rockwell's 'America.'"

When he escaped to the University of Colorado, he drank, chased girls, and skied. In the late 1950s, like a lot of people, he also watched too many Ingmar Bergman movies and read too much Jean-Paul Sartre. "It was very fashionable to read Oriental religion and existentialist literature and smoke a pipe and grow a beard and wear a turtle-neck sweater and really get into the angst. When I went to see Ingmar Bergman films, I wallowed in that old great, self-pity," he recalls, laughing, enjoying the memories. All the while he was battling against the Christianity he learned at home, with its emphasis on an anthropomorphic God who was always "out there," separate from the world.

Partly through the inspiration of American thinker Ralph Waldo Emerson, another former Unitarian minister who became better known as an essayist, Fulghum was drawn to the open-ended spirituality of the Unitarian Church, where atheists and agnostics gather on Sundays alongside Christians and Buddhists. Fulghum's genius lies in finding novel, colorful, everyday images to express universal truths. He attributes some of that common touch to Star King seminary in Berkeley, California, an experimental Unitarian school. Because the seminary's teachers considered him wet behind the ears, they ended up giving him three credits for work he'd found as a bartender.

"They thought, 'This is wonderful. You're green. You don't know much about life. You're going to learn a lot more as a bartender than we can teach you in a classroom. When it's no longer fruitful, we'll stop.' I did it for three years. And it's true. I know more about peoples' troubles and sorrows, because everybody thinks bars are full of drunks, but they're not. They're full of love and lonely people and very funny people. It was a very humanizing experience." Later, he spent time as a mental-health worker, as a San Quentin prison staff member, and in a shelter for the poor. He's also been a cowboy, a folksinger, and a teacher of visual arts. In this last profession he tried to get his students in touch with their imaginations by working, as he does, through their dreams. "No job is mundane," he says, "unless you let it be."

His extroverted zaniness continues to this day. He'll hop in his car, set the odometer at 100 miles, and when it dwindles to zero, step out and talk to anyone he encounters. He has had teenaged art students build sculptures out of wooden matches, then set them alight. "It's a spiritual lesson. The whole of existence is fireborne," he says, revealing both the heart of a poet and the pyromaniacal impulse of a youngster. When he does the laundry at home, he sometimes sticks the static cling-magnetized socks all over the clothes he is wearing.

As for his theology, he's made a big shift from his parents' Christianity. Rather than thinking God is "out there," Fulghum picked up from Eastern thought the idea that there is no place God is not. "God is immanent. God is at all places at all times. So if you think that, it's no longer an issue whether you think Jesus was the son of God. We're all sons of God. We are in the dimension of the extraordinary. I can't imagine Jesus actually sat around thinking, 'Am I really God or am I not? Am I divine or am I not?' You have to say Jesus was a whole man or he was nothing. And if he was a whole man, then he went to the bathroom, he had problems with his teeth, he farted, he told jokes, he even had to have sexual urges. And, if he didn't, then he wasn't a whole human being. People don't want to recognize that aspect of Jesus." He acknowledges that his mother, who died in the early 1990s, felt right up to the end that she'd failed her son by not inculcating in him proper Christian doctrine.

"If you're to stay with the Christian framework, which sees Jesus as both fully God and fully human, then if he didn't know what it was like to struggle with life like I do, then how could he save me from anything? But if he was a man like me, then the story becomes even more profound. Jesus was probably the most provocative teacher of all time."

However, Buddha is as central to Fulghum as Jesus. He keeps a statue of a Buddha in a book-filled room in his waterfront studio, on an altar that also holds a can of Campbell's soup, rocks, an animal skull, feathers, and a can of Spam. The altar, which he says he constantly changes and adapts, serves to acknowledge those things in life that he believes deserve to be talked about. One reason he put the Buddha statue on the altar was that it shows Buddha taking a nap. "I've never heard of Jesus taking a nap," he says. "I am very much mixed in my mind about Buddhism's passive mysticism and Western evangelical activism. Buddhism says ultimately nothing makes any difference. Why sweat it? But Buddhism also says, on the day to day, everything counts. So I have these impulses in my soul that are contradictory." His words tumble out in a broad Texan style.

"Some days I would like to be a Buddhist and fold up into a little ball and become a cultured man. But that goes alongside the value that I ought to be out there for our children, kicking and gouging for people in the future." He can't sit on the sidelines. He remembers seeing the cathedral in Chartres and thinking of the French townspeople who had spent centuries building the wondrous edifice, even though they knew they would never see it completed. "I realized," he says, "I reap what I have not sown."

He believes everyone should get involved in the political process, for instance. "Everybody has obligations because they're citizens. When an election comes along, you gotta be backing candidates. You gotta be going door to door. If you know a bit of history and don't know people have to get involved, then you missed a history lesson. That doesn't make people comfortable any more because it sounds as if you're being very moralistic. But I don't care what people say. It's good what you think, but I want to know what you do! I want to know what you'll settle for. If you'll settle for less than half the American people voting in any old politician, then you know you gotta deal with me!" he growls. He's smiling, but he's not joking.

Nevertheless, he generally prefers to look for what unites people, not what separates them. He knows life is trouble; life is dangerous. But he is an optimist. "The good side of the media is you find out what's going on. The bad side is it's all negative. You never see a headline saying, '200,000 people traveled safely and comfortably today.'" Other than increasingly polluted air and rivers, he believes the world is in better shape now than it's ever been.

Easy for him to say, I politely suggest — after all, he's rich, famous, free to do what he wants. At one time, he says he was nervous about his success; he compares it to a bottomless box of chocolate-chip cookies. But he seems to have avoided overindulging. "I would like to contribute. I would like to end up sitting on the end of my grave and saying, 'Well, I didn't win the Nobel Prize, and I didn't win the Pulitzer Prize, but I won the Refrigerator Award,'" he says, referring to all the people who tell him they cut out his bits of wisdom and stick them on their fridges. "I'd like to think I left a lot of people thinking that they had company in the world, that they were not as alone as they thought they were."

Despite being catapulted into fame, he's determined not to lose touch with what matters: wife, children, the social contract, the guy working at the gas station. "The ultimate issue," he says, "is how I treat my neighbor."

Near the table where he writes, he keeps a sheet of plain white paper tacked to the wall. It takes up a good part of the wall. It is, he says, the most important thing in the room. "What does it profit a man," it says, quoting Jesus, "if he gains the whole world, and loses his own soul?"

Sylvia Fraser

PETER BREGG

"I like mystery. But I don't like secrets."

In her ethereal, all-white apartment in downtown Toronto, Sylvia Fraser is fuming colorfully over a gossip column published in the *Toronto Star*. In it, a radio host has resurrected a cliché put-down, labeling Fraser the "Shirley MacLaine of the North." Many similar arrogant journalists, Fraser says, have dismissed her look at Plato, Einstein, and her own paranormal experiences in *The Book of Strange: A Thinking Person's Guide to Psychic Phenomena.*

On the other hand, the U.S. version of *The Book of Strange*, re-named *The Quest for the Fourth Monkey*, won the American Library Association Booklist Prize. More importantly, the appreciative calls and letters from ordinary people who have had their own psychic experiences keep flooding in. "I have been absolutely touched by the depth of the stories people have told me," she says. "People have been trained to eliminate their experiences and they are grateful for some kind of intelligent interpretation of them. The spiritual revolution that is taking place is better understood by ordinary people than by the media and the heavily educated."

"The media miss all the real social revolutions," she continues. She points out that the media had no idea the Berlin Wall would fall. They didn't know the sexual revolution was arriving. "And now they're playing catch-up on the revolution of pent-up spiritual curiosity." Although Fraser is an acclaimed writer of fiction and nonfiction, she is not immune to sniping from the *Star*, where she worked in the 1960s. Many journalists, Fraser says, speaking rapidly, hardly needing to be prompted by questions, act as if she is excessively gullible about such things as telepathy, prophecy, reincarnation, possession, and meaningful dreams.

Actually, she says, it is the journalists who are gullible. They have failed to question the outmoded worldview they soaked up in high-school science. "Sometimes a little learning is a dangerous thing. I'm quite disgusted by the arrogance of the ill-informed media. The media thought they were being skeptical about my book. But I was the one being skeptical. They were the believers. They were blindly accepting all the old stuff they were taught in school." After all, she points out, school is where most of us learned about Sir Isaac Newton's mecha-nistic view of the universe — a view that was long ago rejected by leading scientists.

Newton taught that the universe is made up of particles — hard little chunks of matter. But twentieth-century physicists such as Paul Davies and biologists such as Charles Birch now tell us the atom is 99.99 percent energy. In other words, says Fraser, reality is not made up of matter, but of energy events. Everything in the universe is alive, pulsing with mind. The post-Newtonian worldview Fraser outlines in *The Book of Strange* is key to justifying her openness to paranormal experiences, whether friendly ghosts or meaningful coincidences. The book's title is inspired by a quote from Einstein: "The Universe is stranger than we imagine."

Fraser's decision to reveal her wide-ranging receptivity to the paranormal follows a life of tumult. As a child, she attended Livingston United Church in Hamilton with her socially respected father and mother, who did not allow smoking, drinking, or taking the Lord's name in vain. After that apparently stolid upbringing, Fraser went on to write five acclaimed novels, including *Pandora's Box*, about a troubled childhood, *Berlin Solstice*, about the Second World War from the Nazi point of view, and *The Emperor's Virgin*, about ancient Roman debauchery. Acclaimed writer Margaret Laurence judged her books "moving beyond words," while poet Irving Layton called them "courageous," and "brilliant."

It was not until the 1980s that Fraser realized why her novels were rife with violent sex. She uncovered buried memories of sexual abuse by her father throughout her childhood. This realization also helped Fraser understand much of her personal life: her divorce, and why she never had children. She detailed the abuse with harrowing honesty in *My Father's House*, which became an international bestseller and has been translated into six languages.

In 1992, with *The Book of Strange*, Fraser made another risky, some say foolhardy, leap. She tried to build a bridge between skeptics and spiritual phenomena by exposing her own paranormal experiences in what she hoped was a serious way, buttressed by science and philosophy.

The night before her mother's funeral, for instance, she describes sleeping in the house occupied by her mother's family for seventy years. That morning, she awakens before dawn "awash in the wakeful expectancy I associate with the dislodging of real secrets. As I lie in that twilight zone between waking and sleep, dream images slide through my consciousness." She sees a baby boy buried in the basement, where she has already felt a "hot spot" on the floor. Weeks later, a cousin tells her of a maternal aunt who used a coathanger to abort a male fetus in that house.

Fraser's King Street West apartment holds many clues to her journey into buried memories, mysticism, and the paranormal. "People tell me being here is like being in the clouds," she says. She is wearing white tights over her thighs, a white blouse, white earrings, a white bracelet, and a white watch. Like many people who have lived sordid lives, Fraser says, she likes white because it requires one constantly washing one's hands. It is also a serene color, symbolic of eternity. Fraser collects glass objects, displaying them on glass tables. "Something about the transparency of glass and crystal appeals to my mind. I like mystery, but I don't like secrets." Walking over her white carpet in bare feet, her bare calves still in shape through cycling, her toenails red, she cheerily points out animal sculptures — dragons, monkeys, cats, panthers, snails, fish, birds — that carry both personal and totemic meaning.

Fraser is still having experiences like those she described in *The Book of Strange*: incredible coincidences, spiritual healings, and premonitions. She broke her leg a year before this interview and, although the doctor said it would take a year to heal, she used meditation and other mind-body techniques and says she had it fully functioning in five weeks. While she does not believe every strange incident is meaningful, she remains open to the possibility that such occurrences have significance.

"I'm not a believer. I'm a quester." She thinks people such as screen actress and New Age leader Shirley MacLaine may have allowed her brain's creative right hemisphere to run ahead of her analytical left hemisphere. "Instead," says Fraser, "I try to keep the hemispheres in harmony. 'What's your sign?' is no substitute for the Dialogues of Plato. 'Do your own thing' does not equate with a Tibetan monk's lifetime of meditation."

To overcome humanity's habitual, but suspect, way of seeing the world, she looks beyond orthodox science and religion. They do not offer the mystical possibilities suggested by a wave of thinkers, some old, some new, who are now, finally, emerging into prominence, feeding society's rising hunger for mysticism.

Instead of seeing the world as composed of Newton's hard billiard balls of matter, Fraser leans toward a worldview better represented by Gottfried Leibniz's energy fields. "Though Newton is known to every school kid, few have heard of Gottfried Leibniz, the seventeenth-century mathematician who shared with him the invention of the calculus. Yet Leibniz proposed a competing mystical cosmology, based on energy fields, which shows stunning parallels to the latest subatomic theory."

Fraser prefers Plato's mysticism to Aristotle's mechanistic theories of natural causation. "Plato believed that the material world was just the manifestation of a greater psychic reality. This reality contained the abstract 'form' or 'idea' of everything, mental and physical. Although Plato's eternal reality cannot be perceived directly by the senses, it can be grasped by intuition aided by reason. To him, the eternal reality was the source of humanity's loftiest ideals — our concepts of beauty and truth and compassion."

Over Charles Darwin's "doctrine" of natural selection, she prefers his contemporary Alfred Russel Wallace's theory that some sort of intelligent force guides evolution. "While Darwin was elevated to stardom, the cofounder of evolution, Alfred Russel Wallace, was consigned to the dustbin; Wallace's crime was to argue that natural selection and survival of the fittest could not alone explain human consciousness or culture, for which he postulated some designing, shaping spiritual force."

Instead of seeing God as an all-powerful rule-maker, she is intrigued by the philosophical writings of Henri Bergson and Alfred North Whitehead, in which God is part of a process and does not precisely know what will happen tomorrow. The future will be a surprise. "I'm intrigued by the idea that God is in the process of being created — and God would be the totality of that which is created. It gets away from the authoritarian idea of God the lawgiver. You don't need a lawgiver. The laws are built into the stuff of the universe."

And instead of accepting the traditional "platitudes" about salvation and heaven from Christianity, a religion she believes has lost its spiritual soul and become obsessed with power and politics, she prefers Buddhism's cyclical view of karma and reincarnation. "I see the unfolding of what seems to be purpose in the universe. It seems to be self-evident. I believe the universe is ruled by broad moral strokes. There tends to be rough justice in the world. I see in the lives of my friends rough justice."

Fraser's 1996 novel, *The Ancestral Suitcase*, revolves around paranormal experiences. Yet Fraser keeps her interest in the paranormal in perspective. After all, in the end, she knows that right action and living a purposeful life are ultimately more important than proving or disproving whether paranormal experiences occur. Now in her sixties, with the busiest stage of her life behind her, she is enjoying meditating and pursuing her spiritual goals. She feels good about life and even about growing old — although, with her carefree curly hair, one can still see in her glimpses of the bouncing Hamilton cheerleader of her teens.

"Our society is missing the idea of stages in life," she says in her characteristic strong, firm tone. She does not fear death, the act around which so many paranormal experiences revolve. "We've been trying to prolong youth to a ridiculous extent. The energy and health of youth is nice, but to be told you have youthful content is not necessarily a compliment. I'm excited about retirement, and I don't mean just playing tennis or golf. The idea of retirement as a filling-in of time is appalling to me. You're young as long as your mind stays active."

The anger sparked by the *Star* column has completely evaporated by the end of the afternoon. She calls her earlier mood atypical of the peace and direction she generally feels. "I know where I'm heading," she says, "and I seem to have a lot of company."

Loreena McKennitt

PETER BATTISTONI

"You put yourself through mental gymnastics so you can go to the performance with as clean a psychological state as you possibly can. . . . But I actually cannot make a spiritual experience happen."

Melancholy tinges Loreena McKennitt's music, say many reviewers. But that word may be too secular. The mood she creates on stage, with flowing red hair brushing up against her Celtic harp, is more spiritually attuned than psychologically morose. With her chanting voice and mesmerizing rhythms, this rising Canadian performer elicits a beautiful aching with her songs, a quiet longing for mystical union that takes listeners to a place that is deeper than it is sad — a place as serene and inspiring as a medieval cathedral or a desert mosque.

Each time McKennitt performs her compositions on stage, she knows there is an opportunity to experience God. But the experience of the presence of the divine doesn't always happen during her shows, which enthral sold-out audiences across North America and Europe. "Those kinds of moments are more visitations, because it's not like you can conjure them up on will alone," she says over dinner in an outdoor restaurant in downtown Toronto. The comment indirectly explains the title of her breakthrough album, *The Visit*.

The Visit won McKennitt a Juno Award and went on to make her an international star, acclaimed in the United States, Britain, Germany, Spain, Italy, and elsewhere. In five years her albums have sold well over one million copies. Open-minded, noncoercive spirituality has been a key to McKennitt's life and music ever since she was growing up under the expansive Prairie skies in the small town of Morden, Manitoba, where she played the organ at St. Paul's United Church for a few years in high school.

"Because I'm a very inquisitive and non-clubby sort of person, it was probably best that my family was connected with a more liberal church. It was very resonant. It laid for me a liberal frame of mind, which I continue to believe in." We meet at a Greek restaurant, just two blocks away from where McKennitt used to busk for a living during the 1980s. She has come to Toronto from her home in Stratford, Ontario, to follow up some music-business details. As she speaks, she reaches into her tumbling hair to finger her earrings, which are shaped like salamanders. She wears a black shawl over her bare, freckled shoulders. She shows no hint of sadness.

She is grateful to the United Church, and to her parents, for their generosity of spirit, she says. (Her father, a livestock trader, died in 1992. Her mother, Irene, lives on Saltspring Island in British

Columbia.) She feels lucky to have been led as a youth to a spiritual path not fueled by negative energy. "I never really went through rebellion in relation to the United Church. But my curiosity has certainly taken me beyond the United Church," she explains. She now rejects the traditional concept that God is a being, like a man with a beard — although many United Church members and other Christians no longer have such an image, either.

With the precision of a philosopher or theologian, McKennitt offers her own definition of God: "A dynamic embodied in the natural world, which manifests itself in the unpredictability and the wonder of nature." Her characterization of God as a creative "dynamic" rather than a being results from a serious study of the ancient roots of Christianity, original religious texts, and world faiths.

But McKennitt is less interested in defining God than in making herself available to the possibility of experiencing God, as is the wont of many musicians. "The only conclusion I can come to is that humans have a need to be spiritually engaged," she says. Experience to her, as to many musicians, counts more than rationality.

To describe how she prepares for that experience, McKennitt brings up the title of another one of her albums, the best-selling *The Mask and the Mirror*. "Many religions 'mask' divinity through unnecessary hierarchy, dogma, and rigidity," she says. She favors the experiential approach of the Sufis, the mystics within Islam, who use the analogy of polishing "the mirror of the soul" to better reflect divinity. "You strive to a kind of perfection that will ultimately result in the union of that essence we call God."

She is not tremendously interested in experiencing God through paranormal phenomena. She is more concerned with solemnity, which, she is quick to point out, doesn't mean sadness, but contains an element of serenity, even celebration. *The Mask and the Mirror* is solemn in a complete sense, which encompasses joy, energy, and spine-tingling awe. *The Mask and the Mirror* explicitly documents McKennitt's own spiritual explorations, which have included study of Celtic mysticism, the Gnostic gospels, and Arthurian legends. The album also includes songs based on poems by St. John of the Cross and W. B. Yeats, and accounts of visits to Spanish holy places and Quebec's Benedictine monastery.

"I think it's really important that more of us develop a sense of our collective histories and how they have influenced each other, and maybe develop more of a tolerance and an understanding of each other," she says. The eclectic album resonates with McKennitt's textured, seductive voice, as well as with droning Gregorian chants, complex Middle-Eastern and Celtic beats, sweeping string instruments, raging bazoukis, and fiery electric guitars.

She doesn't know why people like her music so much. But she receives appreciative letters from a diverse audience that includes neo-pagan witches, Hindus, Catholic nuns, rock 'n' rollers and archeology professors. "All I know is that I get tons and tons of mail from people expressing some sort of spiritual sentiment. I've tried to figure out why it works for them, but I don't know. There seems to be some element to do with the emotion or the passion of it."

Although McKennitt believes she is still at the beginning of her spiritual journey, it would be a mistake to dismiss her metaphysical thoughts as those of an airy-fairy New Ager. A tomboy in her youth, McKennitt is now a tough-minded woman approaching her forties. Her handshake is solid. Her hands feel almost rough, muscled from plucking the thick strings of her harp. She wears bold silver jewelry. In person she has a look less moody, misty, and ethereal than in some of her promotional shots. Her face is hardy.

McKennitt keeps up on world politics, including the European

Union and the divisive internecine battles of the Irish, whose music shaped her.

She follows the cooperative ethics of her rural parents, saying, "I really miss being a part of a community. I think it's important to participate. To do nothing is an overtly political statement." She fights local heritage-building battles. And the day before we met she had gone to the newspaper serving her Stratford home to declare her support for a group of old-order Mennonites, who don't use cars, that had been forbidden to use their horses on the local streets. "Even starting a letter-writing campaign to a newspaper is all related to my beliefs. I don't think people can separate their politics and their religion. It's important to me to take a holistic approach to life — to work with some degree of honesty and collective awareness."

While McKennitt says she doesn't place a high value on material success, emphasizing instead being a good "custodian" of her talent, she understands business better than most business people. Only five years ago she was learning survival skills while busking in Toronto's St. Lawrence Market. "You're very vulnerable when you're busking, because there's nowhere to hide if people don't like you. As it happened, enough people did stop to listen and it gave me a lot of confidence. It also gave me the financial resources to get out of poverty." Sometimes she made $700 in a weekend. But the cash was it; no company would allow her a credit card. Nevertheless, she used the money she had to begin creating her own record company, Quinlan Road. When she finally joined forces with a major record label in the early nineties, she negotiated a better contract than other artists because she already had her own production and distributing outlet.

There is a downside to her take-charge approach to life. It can be hard to polish the mirror of your soul for a performance when, ten minutes before going onstage, you are on the telephone from Germany to New York making a marketing decision. Nevertheless, she believes she owes it to her audience to be ready for that possible visit of the divine. "Sometimes you can't shake off the residue of the day. And you put yourself through mental gymnastics so you can go to the performance with as clean a psychological state as you possibly can. I've amazed myself at how quickly I can switch it over. But I actually cannot make a spiritual experience happen."

The noisy sidewalk restaurant where we talk seems the opposite of the kind of atmosphere McKennitt claims to need to feel whole. Yet spiritual engagement can come through intimate meetings across a dinner table with friends or relatives, she says. And of course it comes through music. But it especially comes through nature. "I would say nature is a tremendously mystical resource. Nature is really the home turf for me spiritually." A bus rumbles by our table, and she raises the volume of her lilting voice to be heard.

Two years ago McKennitt bought a heritage farmhouse, built in 1837, in Stratford. The week before our interview, she helped two baby red-tailed hawks that had fallen out of their nest. One died, but she found another a warm spot and nurtured it to health with a homeopathic remedy.

Most of her "crazy" life, however, is spent on the road or in recording studios. "It's fascinating," she says, "what assumptions people sometimes imagine about me sitting around with my harp. My life is actually the antithesis of that. And I think that's why my specific need for the country is so strong. I spend a dangerously little amount of time in the country or in the natural world that feeds me."

After one gin and tonic and a light meal of Greek food, dusk is falling in the big city and McKennitt is much more relaxed and animated than when the conversation started. She seems engaged. She really needs to be outdoors, she says, even in roaring downtown

Toronto. "When I'm on tour, I always try to stay in hotels that are close to the park, or to the beach. I am completely aware of how integral nature is to my well-being on tour, when I feel really starved, even just to experience temperature changes."

She comments that some cultures, both pre-Christian and modern, have been very connected to nature. She admires the way people of those cultures experienced the divine, rather than pontificated about it. "They felt its rhythms, felt its dynamics. I just feel we've removed ourselves so far from the natural world. To me it's like relearning a lost art and I cherish it very, very much. I mean I love planting flowers around the house, that I smell at different times of day. To me that's sensual. I think nature is tremendously sensual. Very, very sensual." Her voice becomes soft, almost dreamy.

Does she see God as part of nature's sensuality?

"Oh, absolutely. Absolutely."

She laughs, with a warm hum. She uses many words to describe the sense of divinity she obtains from nature. Encompassing. Life-giving. Full.

And sexy. "Using my own instincts and my own feelings as a litmus test," she says with a smile and a chirp, "I would say, yeah, nature's pretty sexy."

A far cry from melancholic.

Farley Mowat

"I believe in God in probably the same way my dog does."

It's fitting that Millicent, a black Labrador, is the first to gambol out to greet me as Farley Mowat, with a smile, walks a few paces behind. At Mowat's old Nova Scotia farmhouse, it soon becomes clear that he puts animals at the forefront of his life. Where others tend to experience divinity in nature as a whole, Mowat's more specific kinship with animals shapes his complex worldview, as can be seen in his more than thirty best-selling books.

Mowat sees the world through the eyes of animals, from the owls and white rats he kept as a child on the Prairies, to the injured birds and gophers he and his wife, Claire, have nursed back to health, to the deer and blue herons that surround his rocky, forested Cape Breton summer property. In the living room of his white house, which is perched above the open, mighty Atlantic Ocean, Millicent slumps contentedly on an oval rug near the wood stove, while Claire, an author in her own right, pops in and out of the book-filled room.

Over coffee, as Mowat discusses the lessons of war, ecological catastrophe, goodness, the centrality of love, the role of religion, his admiration for Jesus, his attitude to death, his belief in the paranormal, and the nature of God, he nearly always comes around to showing how his views are influenced by how an animal might relate to each subject. He has studied and written about animals for fifty years in children's books, hard-hitting essays, and adventures, such as *Never Cry Wolf*, which became a popular movie. No stranger to controversy, he is often cited as a key founder of North America's environmental movement.

Mowat generally prefers animals to humans, a fact that makes him an extreme example of those mystics, writers, and artists who deem nature, rather than book-based religion, to be their greatest source of spiritual teaching. Animals justify Mowat's convictions about God, love, community, the paranormal, and democratic socialism.

Mowat discovered the extent of the human capacity for depravity during the Second World War, and has treated the subject in several of his books, including the bestseller *And No Birds Sang* and the recent *Aftermath: Travels in a Post-War World*. "The war certainly had an enormous impact on me," he recalls. "It opened my eyes. It stripped away the scales and gave me a clarity I might never have had otherwise. The raw reality of what my own species was like and could do was a black revelation."

Instead of blaming or rejecting God in the midst of such suffering, he put the blame where it belonged: on humans. Mowat believes the human animal may soon destroy itself. During bouts of pessimism — which he would simply call "neutralism," or seeing the world as it truly is — he sometimes thinks the best thing the human species could do for the globe's plants and animals is to self-destruct immediately. Humans, he says, have become megalomaniacs. "We've come to believe we can do anything. We are the masters. We have the power." Typically, his sentences are punchy and short. His small, broad-shouldered, tough-looking body, now in its mid-seventies, echoes his blunt, cantankerous, prophetic style.

Mowat is furious about the advertiser-driven promotion of "witless consumption." Humans have lost touch with the need to live within the limits of their environment, he says. Witness, among many ecological catastrophes, the ravaged fish stocks of Canada's East Coast, which he wrote about in 1984 in *Sea of Slaughter*. Now salmon are disappearing from the West Coast.

Mowat calls himself a "small-c" conservative — not, perish the thought, a political Conservative, which he defines as the rich looking out for the rich — because he thinks our species needs to conserve and respect the order found in nature.

He believes nature and animals are essentially good. "I see almost nothing that can be described as evil in the natural world." There is no bloodletting or killing in nature, he says, except for a vital purpose, usually for preservation. "If something is overtly engineered by another entity, then it's a bad thing. That's the way humans do it. We kill people without rhyme or reason. We wage wars. It's abnormal. It's unnatural, because it doesn't occur in nature."

Unlike humans, animals respect nature's built-in restraints. So does the traditional culture of the Inuit, about whom Mowat wrote his first book in 1952, *People of the Deer*. Readers have since bought more than fourteen million copies of his books, which have been translated into fifty-two languages, making him arguably Canada's most widely read author. "The Inuit are going to hate me for this," he says, taking a drag from his cigarette. "I believe they lived as natural animals in a natural world. And they obeyed the restraints and restrictions that nature imposed. They were good animals. Once you escape from those constraints, as we have escaped, you begin to degenerate." His work has always shown respect for natives, the Inuit, and others who face adversity — people who live with what nature throws at them, rather than try to overcome nature so they can be comfortable (and out of touch).

Mowat comes by his old-fashioned, preachy style, full of judgment and warning, honestly. Two of his great-grandfathers were Presbyterian clergymen. "I think that's where he gets all his notions of banging the pulpit," Claire says. Some biographers have said Mowat is not a religious man. "I am a *very* religious man," he insists. Had he been born a hundred years earlier, he thinks he would have been a preacher. But now, as a renowned storyteller, he knows he has a mighty big pulpit from which he can admonish, lampoon, condemn, and exhort.

The Mowats attend a small Anglican church, called St. Mark's, about once a month when they are at their winter home of Port Hope, Ontario. They don't usually go to church during their summer months spent at the 125-acre Cape Breton property, which they intend to leave for posterity as a nature trust. When he's at church, Mowat says, "I even recite the Lord's prayer." Not that he buys all orthodox Christian doctrine. He goes to church, rather, because he believes that every animal, including humans, needs rituals to be reminded of their connectedness to their tribe and world. He thinks ceremonies tie us to each other. "I say the Lord's prayer like I sing 'God Save the Queen,'" he says. "It's part of the ritual approach. If I was in Central Africa, and had some words to say as part of the ritual, I would say it."

Claire, a warm person who is not afraid to take on Mowat when she thinks he gets carried away, tries to clarify that her husband is more a "spiritual person" than a religious person, because he doesn't conform to institutional beliefs. Claire is right. Mowat dislikes conventional religion as much as he dislikes conventional atheists, whom he says often base their atheism on being against things. "Anti-positions," he says, "are suspect if they're vehement." When I tell him of W. P. Kinsella's anger toward the Catholic Church, Mowat says he was once anti-Catholic himself, but considers it an early stage in development. "You grow out of that. You get to the place I'm at now, where the Catholic Church is something you recognize exists for a reason. It has many aspects I deplore; so has every other religion. But to be a virulent anti-Catholic is a waste of time and energy."

Mowat certainly doesn't talk about God in a traditional church way. "I believe in God in probably the same way my dog does, or the seagull flying over there does." He gestures at Millicent, and at the birds riding the foggy air currents over the gray Atlantic.

Mowat doesn't want to define God. He thinks it's human arrogance to try. "I don't need to bash my head against the little walls of our human cell and say, 'I've gotta write this down. I've got to give it shape and color and form.' Why not just accept it?"

When Claire jokes that "he'll never get to be archbishop," Mowat responds, "I just know an exercise in futility when I see it."

What people call God, Mowat says, is a motivation, a cause, a condition of existence, for all things. "Somewhere something, or some combination of things, seems to be providing direction. It's so difficult to grasp. And I think our tiny minds, which we think are so wonderful, are quite incapable of grasping this. I can live with an amorphous awareness that this whole universe cannot possibly be an accident. I can live in the void of simply recognizing there is a force, without trying to define it."

Mowat calls the claim that Jesus is divine "nonsense." Yet, he admires Jesus as "a gifted teacher with good ideas, a prophet, an individual with great perceptivity, and a socialist revolutionary, of course." He regrets that the socialist experiment has never been given a full chance to succeed, taken over by dictators in places such as Russia and squeezed out of other regions by external forces.

Launching into a complicated analysis of the history of the Balkan region, Mowat says Western powers helped start the war in the former Yugoslavia by meddling in former president Tito's successful state, which was "communism with a benign face." When Croatia tried to break away from Yugoslavia, Mowat maintains it was like Quebec trying to leave Canada and then getting supported by the United States. "If that happened, the rest of Canada would think, 'How dare you!' And when the rest of Canada rose up to protect our country by military means, the United States would call in the United Nations and provide safe havens for Quebec and surreptitiously provide Quebec with weaponry while putting an embargo on Canada and sending in peacekeepers. It's the same story."

He also finds it fascinating that some former Communist countries, such as Hungary, have voted to return to Communism, and even more interesting that the Western media basically aren't reporting on it. "What you can conclude from that with a fair degree of accuracy is that Hungarian communism must be working. If it wasn't working, we'd be hearing about it."

Jesus, he says, understood what it was like to be a good socialist animal. Jesus knew all the earth's creatures are linked, belonging to one another and relying on each other. "Jesus said it all. He said

'We're all in the same boat.' He said 'Throw out the moneylenders. We must look after each other. We have to be decent. We have to be relatively honest.' All the things Christ preached are first-rate philosophical concepts."

The trouble is, he says, humans now think they control their own destiny. They're ignoring wise teachings such as those of Jesus, and taking too many liberties with the laws of nature that link us together. "All forms of life are interrelated. I don't care what any religious organization, or any intellectual organization, says about it. They're talking doubletalk. We're all part and parcel of the same entity. And that knowledge gives me the strength to go on, watching my own race, my own species, disintegrate. I can handle it with equanimity. If I didn't believe that I was an essential part of the whole stream of life, then I'd go out of my wits with what we're doing. Hope doesn't lie with us. It lies beyond us. It lies in life itself."

He feels sustained, he says, mainly by his connections with nature, especially other animals. "I can go for a walk and encounter another animal — *another* animal, notice, not an animal, but *another* animal — and something about its behavior strikes me with warmth. It gives me a warm feeling, a sense of being part of its world and it being part of mine. I feel comfortable."

"Feels" is the operative word. Mowat believes humans have vastly overrated the importance of thinking. "I have a deep, deep abiding mistrust for the intellect. It's the worm within that is busy destroying us." Our rational minds, he feels, have mostly got us into trouble. It's part of the reason he doesn't try to define God. "In my seventy-odd years, I've found rationality a false doctrine. To trust the rational over the emotional is to risk annihilation." What's important, he says, is that everything, including animals and nature, feels. "I feel, therefore I am."

Mowat calls this phrase just another of his weird ideas. But some eminent philosophers and biologists, such as Australian Charles Birch, say the same thing. They are part of a school of thought called *pan-experientialism*, which counters the dominant idea that the world is a machine. While many influential philosophers such as René Descartes have proposed that only humans have feelings, the late twentieth-century Harvard philosopher and mathematician Alfred North Whitehead writes: "In animals we can see emotional feeling, dominantly derived from bodily functions, and yet tinged with purposes, hopes, and expression." Panexperientialism says living entities in the universe — humans, animals, atoms — have unified feeling. Even thoughts themselves, according to Whitehead and Birch, are "intellectual feelings." While most of us have missed this point, opting for a mechanistic view, Mowat's fascination with biology has kept him in tune with how feelings connect us all.

Our rational, mechanistic mindset, according to Mowat, has contributed toward our complete capitulation to the allure of technology. Since the advent of the steam engine, perhaps earlier, he says, rising technology has been causing our species to lose its basic functions. "There's a law which is the law of functions. No form of life continues to have viability if it loses function. And what we have done with our technological inventiveness is deprive many of us of our ordinary normal functions, removing them off to machines to do them for us. From the automobile up, from the steam engine up, the loss of function is what dooms the human being. Old people, when they lose function, go to pieces. Our species, as we continue to lose function as a viable animal, will also go to pieces and then disappear. Probably most of our brains will become irrelevant. The computers will be doing it for us. The computer is increasingly taking over the amassing of information and processing. Artificial intelligence, which some people are in awe of, is a death sentence."

He smiles. He is enjoying the chance to try to shock the world awake. Mowat offers a drink for a second time; I decline because of the long drive back to Halifax. Storm clouds are appearing over the sea and it looks as if I'll be driving through the rain. Claire brings in some coffee and cookies and says she's finding the interview much more "significant" than many she's listened to.

To keep in touch with some of his human functions, Mowat travels to this remote Cape Breton home during deepest winter by himself to do manual household repairs, including carpentry.

Not only have humans, he feels, lost physical and intellectual function, but through overspecialization and excessive rationality we have also lost spiritual function, including the power to communicate at an extrasensory level. Animals appear to communicate through a form of ESP, he says. Most humans have lost it because they've become too civilized.

"But primitive people certainly do have it. There's no question about it." In the late 1940s, just after the war, Mowat was in a cabin with an Inuit man who suddenly became paralyzed with overpowering emotion. "He was receiving a startling piece of information that somebody close to him in the camp had just died an accidental and dramatic death." At the time, the man's friend was fifteen miles away.

"The [extra-sensory] perception of calamity seems to be universal. Most animals have it. And we had it too when we were good animals. It's one of the attributes we had, which has atrophied. It's been replaced with technical invention, like the telephone, but we don't realize it. It's like hearing. A guy who is born deaf doesn't realize he's deaf."

Despite his dwindling hope for humanity, Mowat still believes in the centrality of the greatest feeling in the cosmos, love. "Love is the vital ingredient. It's the glue that may or may not hold us together. It's ingrained. It's not a human attribute alone. You can see it in almost every form of life. There's 'mother love' with practically every so-called higher animal. One would have to assume all kinds of love exist in all animal life."

The capacity for love is a matter of degree, he says. An earthworm, for instance, is not going to be as loving a partner as a whale. In his book *A Whale for the Killing*, Mowat describes a whale expressing love by staying as close as it can to its captured partner for six days, until it dies. Every dog he and Claire have had have certainly enjoyed affectionate, compassionate relationships with humans and other animals. Leaning over to Millicent, Mowat puts two embracing hands around her ears and says, "And you. You're a sucker for love."

Barry Lopez

JEFF VINNICK

*"We're living on a continent where we are obsessed
with being in power, rather than being in love."*

Barry Lopez is speaking about hunting — quietly, lyrically. When a
wild animal is killed with a sense of reverence by a person who treats
the animal's death as a gift rather than a conquest, he says, some native
Indians believe the animal's spirit receives another body to inhabit.
The spirit is then free to wander off again into the world.

His voice is hushed, like a priest speaking to a cherished parishioner.
"I initially saw death in nature as the taking of life," he says. "But it is

199

not the *taking* of life if it's received as a gift. People who are always posing questions of power, rather than questions of love, are the ones who speak of the *taking* of life."

Lopez keeps his voice low because he doesn't want to impose himself on the other diners in the tiny Vancouver restaurant. He speaks as if he's in a cathedral. In many ways, the entire world is Lopez's cathedral. His eyes, narrow-set, intense, and probing, have a look of animal readiness. He wears a native turquoise bracelet, a gold wedding ring, and a tightly clipped gray beard that has endured extremes of cold, heat, and natural forces most dare only to imagine.

Lopez is the author of *Arctic Dreams: Imagination and Desire in a Northern Landscape*, which won the U.S. National Book Award for nonfiction. It is an extensive contemplation on the connection between nature and spirituality, based on five years he spent in Alaska and the Canadian Arctic. In it, he asks the reader to consider the holiness not only of animals, but of icebergs and light.

The context for virtually all of Lopez's writing is the natural world — whether the Canadian Arctic, the Australian outback, Africa, or Nebraska's rivers. As well as *Arctic Dreams*, his works include *Of Wolves and Men* and three collections of short stories: *Desert Notes*, *River Notes*, and *Field Notes*. He has been called a member of the new naturalist school of writing.

Even though he always returns from his travels to Brenda, his wife of several decades, and his rural home on the McKenzie River in Oregon, he offers Canadians, a people who cannot help but be shaped by the vastness of their land, insights on how to experience it. Ironically, he claims that the real subject of his writing is not the wilderness, but love.

These days he is reflecting hard on the meaning of love. He thinks about it like a scholastic monk from an indeterminate religion. Love seems to offer the link that could tie together his ever-evolving, Earth-revering worldview. He defines God as "the fullest expression of the mystery we call love."

Asked about the planet's future, he answers that it is threatened because "we're living on a continent where we are obsessed with being in power, rather than being in love."

Except, perhaps, for ecological theologians such as Sallie McFague, herself an admirer of Lopez, there is perhaps no writer today who has put more effort into reflecting on the spiritual insights offered by nature. In *The Rediscovery of North America*, Lopez developed a key metaphor for human disregard for nature: the image of Spanish conqueror Hernando Cortés setting fire to Mexico City, burning the orchards, flowers, and aviaries of what some say was the most beautiful city in the world. Cortés wanted to tame the land and its people. Although Lopez avoids the label of political writer, his work amounts to a call to righteous anger against the ongoing destruction of land by a relatively small number of people who are bent, not on surviving, but on amassing wealth and power.

Lopez's sense of respect for life, human and non-human, seems to have penetrated every cell of his body. But his philosophy has been refined over the years. Born in 1945, he was raised in California's San Fernando Valley, where he nurtured his sense of oneness with nature by raising pigeons. He hasn't seen his natural father since he was three. When his mother, a school teacher "who held everything together," moved to the eastern United States, he attended a Jesuit high school, then Notre Dame University, where he studied Western philosophy — epistemology, metaphysics, logic, and esthetics — as well as engineering, physics, and biology. At age twenty-one, he entered the seminary with plans to become a Catholic priest.

The day he left the Trappist monastery defines his worldview, which he now calls "small-c" catholic. Lopez remembers reading in a court-yard at the Abbey of Gethsemani in Kentucky, once the home of the famous Christian-Buddhist philosopher Thomas Merton. "The important thing about Gethsemani," he recalls, "is it was very earth-oriented. I remember coming down the stairs and seeing this beautiful oak floor covered with rubber boots. Cotton workjackets were the common clothes the monks wore in mass. They were a group of working-class men whose lives were devoted to physical labor and spiritual attentiveness. I couldn't imagine a more perfect life."

But he decided to leave one day after looking through a gate to the outside world. "It was like a medieval gate suggesting the separation of the sacred and profane. And as I looked at the monks in gumboots and cotton gloves, in that moment, I realized it was so perfect it couldn't be right. Whatever my work was was not there. The love of God seemed a cornerstone of life. The question for me was: What does this mean? For a long time that meant being religious, then it became spirituality."

Lopez moved to Oregon and wrote his first book when he was thirty-one. Titled *Giving Birth to Thunder, Sleeping with His Daughter: Coyote Builds North America*, it is a collection of native American stories about the transformative trickster, a mythological figure who represents divine qualities of surprise and novelty. "When I discovered the trickster figure, I saw something that was tremendously exciting to me, a character who had been distorted by the process of tearing it out of an indigenous culture." Lopez came to reject orthodox Catholicism. He now believes it is a dogmatic institution dominated by people who think the white, male, Christian viewpoint is the most important. He can't accept how the Catholic Church excludes women from key positions and fails to support Latin American liberation the-ologians who side with the poor. He equates "religion" with people

trying to force other cultures, other people, to agree to one set of beliefs. "I find religion now too narrow an expression of the love of God, and in some instances, I would say too dark and menacing."

He is not exactly opposed to organized religion, but hopes traditional believers would recognize that what is right for them doesn't necessarily have to be right for others. "Religion is a container for spirituality. And no container is adequate. Spirituality is uncontainable."

How does he define "spirituality," that amorphous word that is becoming more popular than "religion," particularly among young people, because of its noninstitutional connotation?

"It is an awareness of, and commitment to, love. Something I've learned as a writer, because of the way I conduct research, I guess, is that you'll find brilliance in every corner. You'll find illumination in every corner. If you go back to the simple life of the historical Jesus, we'll see he spoke to Gentiles, he sat with prostitutes, he saw the possibility of love in every quarter."

Lopez doesn't particularly follow any tradition, although he says his popular mythological tale, *Crow and Weasel*, sums up his worldview. The novella picks up a native theme about young people finding themselves and their role in their community through endurance in the wilderness.

Many people have also told him he takes a Buddhist approach. "But I'm certainly more Christian than I am Buddhist. I admire Jesus because he had the courage to insist on love in a world that is devoted to power. I'm not Buddhist enough to know what they really believe. But I've certainly tried to incorporate Buddhist principles such as *ahimsa*, the principle of not harming [any living being], into my own spiritual beliefs."

Lopez, after all, once surprised North America with a widely distributed article about his lifetime habit of removing dead animals —

roadkill — from highways and back roads. "I do it out of respect. One of the reasons that compelled me was the awareness that the individual animal I removed from the road could have been a spiritual leader or a warrior in its community. So it's a gesture toward the elders of another parallel culture."

Lopez doesn't like being seen as just a writer about nature; nor does he want to make idols of animals, plants, and rocks. But he ponders constantly, looking for epiphanies and moments of wonder. He comes to a realization during our talk, which he says has focused on his spirituality in ways most interviews never do. (Most people ask him about the political implications of his writing.) "I pay a lot of attention to animals," he says, "but what is driving it is as much spiritual curiosity as biological curiosity. I've never quite thought of it that way before."

In his quest, he adds, he is becoming more and more interested in exploring beauty — not just pleasant sunsets, but the *meaning* of beauty, and in particular "moral beauty" in people and the world.

How does his curiosity about beauty connect to his belief in the overarching role played by love? I apologize for asking such an abstract question, which many people would find embarrassing.

"Oh, my, no," he says. "That's really good." He pauses to contemplate his answer. A peaceful silence descends. "I guess I would say that if you see beauty, you know you're in the presence of love."

He pauses again. "I'm drawn continuously to the intersection of beauty and desire and love, all of which seem to coalesce in issues of land."

He is mesmerized by the land and its inhabitants. But he seeks far more than scientific explanations of its complexities. "The most intelligent thing we can do is love," he says, "not reason." He believes the more we converse with nature, the more we learn about what really matters, the more we learn about love. "The world knows we're struggling. It reaches out to us, and we can take advantage of that compassion. What we can learn from the characters in my books, I think, is how crucial it is to pay attention to the world outside ourselves."

Nick Bantock

"Some notions of divine creativity seem to be images of something that comes from above, with some kind of magic wand. I much prefer the idea that it comes from an earthy place that is full of sexuality and sensuality."

Nick Bantock's directions to his home on Bowen Island, a twenty-minute ferry ride from Horseshoe Bay in West Vancouver, were enigmatic at best.

When I drive off the ferry onto Bowen, the first thing I see is a black bear that had long been the fear of the island inside a wildlife officer's cage. Children drinking soda pops from the village store stare through the steel mesh at the drugged creature. I drive up into the island's mountains and towering forest and, after taking a few false turns on a bumpy, twisted route, eventually find Bantock's two-and-a-half-acre enclave and onion-domed house. Bantock is working in a white, dust-free studio that smelled fresh as rain. Two of his four children, all of whom are under the age of twelve, are playing on the mown grass with his artist wife, Kim Kasasian.

I tell him it hadn't been easy finding his place. With a smile on his handsome, bearded, narrow face, he says he tries not to be too pre-scriptive when he gives directions; he wants to give visitors the benefit of the doubt that they can find it themselves.

Bantock's books have the same vaguely disconcerting air of challenge. He is a trickster, a metaphysical puzzle-maker. Inspired by the creative energy of nature, his curiosity leads him to explore every facet of the universe, including its demons. You can only overcome the dark things inside by searching for them and facing them head on, he believes. That way lies balance.

My journey to his hobbit-like property in the heart of Bowen Island, which has about 3,000 residents with homes along its rocky shores and in its forest, seemed like a chance to pick up clues to the mysterious puzzles Bantock poses in his famous *Griffin and Sabine* trilogy, as well as in *The Egyptian Jukebox* (which is literally a riddle, with an answer on the last page) and *The Shiva*.

The *Griffin and Sabine* trilogy, which has sold over two million copies, consists of a mystical correspondence, complete with envelopes and pull-out letters, in which shadowy figures seethe out of an enigmatic landscape. The trilogy loosely follows a famous poem by W. B. Yeats, *The Second Coming*, which many have interpreted as apocalyptic. Bantock bears some similarity to Yeats, who was a romantic, alchemy-loving Irish poet.

But Bantock is impossible to pin down: part Jungian specialist, part

Zen aficionado, part amateur Gestalt therapist, part homeopath, part poet, part visual artist.

The images of his metaphysical puzzles — inspired by such diverse sources as dreams, the unconscious, Egyptian occult religion, astrology, and the cosmos — are as real and vivid to Bantock as the giant fir trees surrounding his home. Facing and declawing inner demons is what Bantock's life is all about; I shouldn't have been surprised, therefore, at his reaction to the news of the capture of Bowen Island's black bear.

"That's too bad," he says. "It added a little spice."

He delights in seeing boundaries pushed. He recalls the time he participated in a guided imagery about bears. During their descent into the unconscious, most people in the group confronted terrifying bears. "But my bear was a talking bear. We had a little chat. And the bear carried on with what he was doing, and I went on my way. There was no problem. I don't think of bears being hostile, unless they're provoked."

It is typical of Bantock that his teeming unconscious would offer up a friendly bear. He sees himself as a modern-day Puck, a trouble-making trickster he once portrayed as a bearlike creature with an ice-cream cone. "I'm just a mischief maker. It's my job to stir the pot." When I tell him that Mordecai Richler, Bill Reid, and Barry Lopez are also drawn to the trickster figure, he says he loves the Navajo trickster known as the *kachina*, "whose job it is to put the coffee cup nearer the edge so you knock it over. I love the idea that the trickster wakes you up by giving you a little shock. If it's too big, it's a trauma. But it's good to have little electric shocks."

If there was any doubt about Bantock's playful, creative fascination with the dark side of reality, it was erased when he took a telephone call and I visited the bathroom on the main floor of his studio. A black-blue painting of a serpent with a rodent-like head hangs directly above the toilet. The forbidding creature seems to be attacking whomever dares use the facility.

I mention it when I get back to the second floor studio, where he keeps paintings, sculptures, and a dizzying variety of books, from *The Guinness Book of Records* to titles about Monet and the blues. I say the bathroom painting seems like a joke, but with a message perhaps about the shadow. Pushing his long fingers through tousled hair, without smiling, he replies, "The more we deny our dark internal side, the more potential it has to control us. Our shadow is dangerous when we don't acknowledge it."

Bantock is anything but forbidding himself, however. With his knees pulled up to his chin, he places his feet on his chair. His wiry body moves like an enthusiastic teenager. In daily life, it is evident, he values kindness, which he considers a lack of malice. But his exterior pleasantness comes from years of interior exploration that has sometimes bordered on frenetic. "I believe my art has always been a way of allowing me to express both sides: my passion for life, but also my awareness of the darkness that is born out of my childhood fears. There is a tendency for this society to say it only likes the light. But when we constantly push down that which we don't like, it is not only exhausting, it is corrupting."

This Jungian theory of light and shadow is key to his philosophy of finding balance; the title of the last book in the *Griffin and Sabine* trilogy is *The Golden Mean*. Aristotle taught that the Golden Mean lies between two extremes. Too much courage, for example, is foolhardiness. Too little courage is cowardice. The Golden Mean is similar to the Buddha's Middle Path, which resides between self-indulgence and self-renunciation.

Bantock grew up in the suburbs of London, England. He was, he admits, a nervous character, a stupendously bored only child whose main question was "Why?" His basic interests — obsessions — were girls and soccer. "I went to Sunday school until I was age thirteen. Church of England. Then I went to some kind of evangelical thing because they had the best soccer team," he laughs. "Soccer for the British and most Europeans is a form of group hooliganism."

He was knocked over by Bill Buford's book, *Among the Thugs*, which is about running with gangs of ultra-violent soccer fanatics in Britain. "It was one of the most scary books I'd ever read because I understood it completely. I was part of that. It brought back all the fears. Soccer can be defined as a religion because it can be so much like an obsession."

By the time Bantock had gone through therapy and become a top illustrator, however, he felt stifled in England. He moved with his wife to British Columbia in 1986. The Golden Mean was becoming a metaphor for his attempts to make peace with the extremes that have always churned inside him.

He easily sees connections beween his everyday realm and the metaphysical realm. For example, he describes how he still plays soccer: "Moments occur in soccer when you forget who you are and you become part of the whole. It's almost like catching the rhythm of totality. For just a few seconds you seem blessed with some kind of magic. And then it's gone, and you're just an ordinary Joe fumbling around with the ball getting thumped in the back of the legs."

He must remain disciplined, he says, to avoid being consumed by sports, either playing them or watching them on TV.

"Achieving balance is an ongoing process. You never completely succeed. All you can do is notice when you've become out of balance. If you're going on a high wire, and you start to think about how high you are, you're going to fall off. What you have to think about is the next step. So, in my daily life, there are times when I feel uncomfortable: I've eaten the wrong food, had an argument, been petulant or made a wrong decision. And that's going to throw me out of balance. The key is to quickly realize that and redress the balance."

He eschews standard religious doctrine. "Doctrine to me is like group support. There are times in your life when you need it, but mostly I don't." Bantock prefers to find guidance through eclectic sources, including Zen Buddhism. He believes that the elusive nature of Zen mysticism epitomizes spirituality. As is the way of the artist, and of the mystic, he employs a telling image to characterize a Zen truth about the ultimate nature of reality: "It's the reflection of the moon in the water. As long as you look, you can see it. But the moment you put your hand into the water, it breaks the moon."

Bantock also cherishes a Zen phrase he once stumbled upon: "The sense in nonsense." Perfect for a Puck, a transformer. "Suddenly I had justification about where humor fits in spirituality. Suddenly I got it." Humor, he says, wakes us up. "It's a way of not taking ourselves too seriously, particularly the kind of humor you call gallows humor. When things are at their worst, then you crack a joke, it's a way of getting some scale between yourself and the size of the universe."

When he speaks, Bantock's language is sharp and rich as the images that emerge from his blast-furnace mind. His London accent, which often drops the "r," is textured and colorful. Words explode out of him, but each one is chosen carefully.

He won't, for example, use the word "God" to describe the focus of his metaphysical high-wire act. The word has become so broadly defined, he says, as to be almost meaningless. "Better not feed people's preconceptions by using it. It's better to call it something else and then define it in a way that feels comfortable. Then you redefine it and redefine it and redefine it."

He prefers the word *duende*, as described by the great Spanish writer García Lorca. "*Duende* is full of passion and vitality," says Bantock. "What it really is is the spirit of the earth coming up through the soles of the feet and filling your body with creative passion." He illustrates, running stretched-out fingers over his body.

"I love *duende* because it's romantic. I love it because it's dramatic. I love it because it's about your responsibility to make things happen." Bantock hates the idea of an all-powerful God who hands out creative ideas on a platter to deserving artists. "Some notions of divine creativity seem to be images of something that comes from above, with some kind of magic wand. I much prefer the idea that it comes from an earthy place that is full of sexuality and sensuality."

I mention that Lorca's *duende* sounds a bit like French philosopher Henri Bergson's *élan vital* and American theologian John Cobb's *creative transformation*, the divine force field that shapes the evolutionary process. Bantock likes the comparison, but quickly adds that *duende* is impish as well. "This is really important. It's quixotic. It doesn't allow you to dwell on your own abilities. If you indulge, then it's gone."

If you indulge in *duende*, it's gone?

"Yes. And the next day it comes back," he says, with a giggle. A visit from the divine is only possible when your soul is rid of clutter and ego.

Another way Bantock has tipped his personal scales to the middle and found balance in life is by staring into his own death. "Very interesting business, death. The first time you ever experience your own mortality is a big shock. For me, it happened about two months before my first child was born, about ten years ago. I remember lying in bed and thinking, 'This thing is going to be born, therefore I'm going to die. Oh my God!' It happened in a flash of a second. I felt like someone had opened a big trap door and I'd seen the whole of the universe in one go. It all rushed in and I was struck with complete and utter panic. I was shaking for days and days. It actually took me about two weeks to get out of the house after that."

He remains skeptical about the existence of life after death, or the reality of Buddhist reincarnation. He considers what happens after death to be more of a curiosity than anything else, because what he thinks about it won't change what happens. But confronting death made him turn his life around. He began living more healthily. He dug more deeply into homeopathy, which centers on building resistance to disease. Homeopathy made him realize spirituality is not about chasing a light out there, but about how you live your life. "It was my first real look at holistic responsibility. Everything you do is part of your spirituality. You can't separate it off. And if you deny it, it's at your peril." Homeopathy shapes Bantock's belief that whatever you do within yourself, on a microscopic level, manifests itself on the macroscopic level. To him, all different spheres of reality, from the unconscious to the cosmological, are related.

Bantock is also open to the notion of synchronicity, the Jungian idea that coincidental events have cosmic significance. His commitment to the idea that all things are interconnected also makes him concerned about extremism — lack of balance — on a global scale. "The interesting thing about homeopathy is you can relate it to the individual or you can relate it to the mass. In the homeopathic sense, if you do not deal with the cause of a disease, the symptom will become bigger and more powerful until you deal with the cause. As humans, we're not looking at the whole: at all people, at the animal kingdom or the Earth. That means we could get continually expanding outbursts of sickness and plagues."

He does not feel as anxious now about the imminent end of the world as he did when he was a teenager and thinking every birthday would be his last. But if the apocalypse comes, he thinks that in this age of pollution, AIDS, increasingly useless antibiotics, and rampaging allergies it could come in the form of the breakdown of the immune system. "We're eroding ourselves on many fronts. And it's not them and us. We are doing it to ourselves. And we have a choice in this matter. Do we do something about it or don't we?"

Bantock admits he has been "excessively evasive" about giving direct answers to readers and journalists who have tried to puzzle out the ambiguous, possibly apocalyptic, meaning of the *Griffin and Sabine* trilogy. But he momentarily forgets his resolve that individual readers should work out their own meaning. He starts by clearing up that, although Griffin and Sabine communicate their thoughts to one another in the book, he doesn't believe in telepathy. Instead, he sees Griffin and Sabine as different personalities within the same person.

And what of the line tucked away on the last postcard in the last book of the trilogy? From Yeats's "The Second Coming," it goes: "And what rough beast . . . slouches . . . to be born." Literary specialists have traditionally interpreted the line as the biblical beast of the Book of Revelation ushering in the end of the world.

Not Bantock. "Throughout his poem," he says, "Yeats talks about how 'things fall apart, the centre cannot hold.' But I didn't see the last line as a kind of horrendous, apocalyptic ending. I saw it much more as a cyclic return."

For Bantock, the poem describes an individual dying and being reborn. "It's like after having an accident, you see the sky and how blue it really is for the first time."

The *Griffin and Sabine* trilogy, he says, is about two parts of the same individual learning to love one another and find reconciliation. It is about finding the Golden Mean. Balance.

He stops, sucks in air. "That's the nearest I've ever come to explaining it. I don't know if I should do it now."

The trickster stares at the ceiling, contemplates. He concludes: "No. No. It's all right because a lot of people aren't going to get it anyway."

Alex Colville

*"I read a lot of existentialist literature in the fifties . . .
One of its ideas was the concept of the absurd, that things
don't make sense. That is completely repugnant to me."*

Few things are more important to Alex Colville than order. When he
was a youngster, Colville, like his steelworker father, respected the
police and their job of keeping the peace. When he served as an artist
for Canada during the Second World War, Colville admired the military hierarchy because an officer's first responsibility was always to his
soldiers. When the war ended, Colville learned to admire the
Germans' serious, systematic way of structuring society. By the time

his precise paintings had made him one of the few artists most Canadians recognize by name, Colville had little time for all those romantic artists who claimed they prized anarchy.

Sitting in a straight-backed chair in the peaceful sunroom of his heritage home in Wolfville, Nova Scotia, Colville says he believes God, if you'd like to call it God, is the source of order in the universe.

"I read a lot of existentialist literature in the fifties: Camus, Sartre, Simone de Beauvoir. It was a movement that had a great effect on my generation. One of its ideas was the concept of the absurd, that things don't make sense. That is completely repugnant to me," he says, placing strong, large-knuckled fingers to his firm chin.

Colville takes the unfashionable position that if God had not helped provide order in the universe, we would not have a universe. Colville finds strong resonances in a neurologist friend's wonder at the complexity and order of the human body's central nervous system. He also values the amazing proportions he finds in trees, landscapes, and animals. "It's the same sense that very ordinary, you might say unlearned, people have, perhaps. I think a learned person is more likely to lose this sense of awe. And I haven't lost it. And I think for me that is my sense of God. I don't see the world as absurd. I see the world as amazingly intricate and amazingly successful. I exclude humans, of course."

Like Farley Mowat, Colville saw human depravity at its worst in the Second World War. Also like Mowat, he finds that animals offer a better moral example. Now in his seventies, his voice still steady and modulated, Colville talks about his two-fold respect for order. He adores the order of nature, and believes humans must show more respect for order if they are to ward off evil. On his fit body he wears white cotton pants and a white shirt buttoned up to the top. His white hair is cut in a vaguely military burr. But the white moccasins he wears without socks, like the frequent nudes in his paintings, hint that he is more than just a stuffed shirt. Comfortable in his large old home, which is decorated with fine, polished antique furniture, he is approachable and attentive.

A gentle man in a gentle land.

He has lived among these rolling green hills, farms, and curving roads since 1929. "It always seems corny, but the sacred in a sense is all around us," he says. He would never think of moving from this idyllic town that houses Acadia University near the Bay of Fundy, where his wife, Rhoda, who appears in many of his paintings, was born. He and Rhoda, who celebrated their fiftieth wedding anniversary in 1992, raised their four children in this region. He believes that the sacred is everywhere, for those who have eyes to see, and is therefore perplexed by people who travel in hopes of finding thrills.

And he wonders why so many twentieth-century artists constantly talk about creating something "exciting." Like an Eastern mystic, he says, he is more attracted to serenity than excitement. The man who has been called "the most important realist painter in the Western world," whose great reputation extends to Germany and other European countries, tries to capture what he calls "moments of meaning" in his quietly tense paintings. His style has been called magic realism. Like the Christian mystic Gregory the Great, Colville paints, wrote his biographer Helen Dow, as if "the aim of art is to render visible the mysteries of the supra-natural world." Colville doesn't disagree.

The complex designs in Colville's paintings, which each take up to six months of calm concentration to produce, are based on patterns and proportions set down by ancient Egyptian geometricians. Like a medieval monk painstakingly illustrating sacred texts, melding meditation and the arts, Colville has no respect for unchained passion. Art, he maintains, cannot be created in chaos. Perhaps intuitively, Colville has ingested into his soul one of the classic insights of theology: that God is the ground of order.

At its worst, such an understanding of God can lead to seeing God as the sanctioner of the status quo, causing an unhealthy deference to religious and political authorities, even dictators. But Colville seems to understand divine order in a sense more like that proposed by twentieth-century philosopher-theologians such as John Cobb and biologists such as Charles Birch, who see God as the ground of a changing and developing order that must continuously incorporate novelty if it is to avoid becoming repressive. Order, in their view, is essential to the maximization of enjoyment, which is God's ultimate purpose for the universe. The human, for example, could not have rich experiences without the order of the body.

On the other hand, excessive order can inhibit enjoyment. Philosopher Alfred North Whitehead speaks of "the contrast between order as a condition for excellence, and order as stifling the freshness of living." Colville's intensely enjoyable, meaningful, accessible works of art perfectly capture a sense of both order and creative novelty.

It is interesting to compare Colville and Mowat. They are both anti-elitist. They both want their work to be enjoyed by typical people, not an esoteric, artistic in-crowd. But despite their many shared views — about creating art for real people, about the horrors of war, about the superiority of animals, and about respect for the order of the natural world — Mowat turned out an in-your-face socialist, while Colville considers himself a conservative — a red Tory, to be precise. When I told Mowat I had visited Colville on the same trip to Nova Scotia in which I saw him, Mowat joked that Colville was a "redneck." But maybe the two aren't that far apart on an ethical plane.

Colville decries classic liberalism. "Speaking in political terms, I see the liberal thing as being essentially middle class, based on the misconception that everyone has equal abilities and everyone could make it if they just kept their act together." When some don't, Colville argues, the liberal just shrugs and says, "I'm all right, Jack. I've got my Oldsmobile."

The real conservative, in Colville's view, is more compassionate. In contrast with much right-wing ideology today, Colville believes that the authentic conservative thinks the rich must take responsibility for the underdog: "The weak are defended by the strong." To promote this ideal, since 1979, Colville has given $1,000 a year to Canada's Conservative Party, even though it doesn't always meet his definition of a classic conservative. He also gave $18,000 to charity last year. He admires the German people because they take seriously their public duties. And although he feels contempt for much government bureaucracy, he admires the German system of balancing state intervention with the market.

Another thing he admires in the German people is that, with Naziism in their recent past, they have realized how bad they can be. "Canadians think we could never do things like that. I don't buy that at all." He thinks people must face their buried capacity for evil. And to really live, they must also look squarely into the face of death. Many people find a sense of unease in Colville's paintings, and he acknowledges that his belief that life is dangerous, and in some ways inexplicable, comes across in his work. That belief is one of the reasons he seeks serenity.

Since Colville's own religious views don't reflect dominant streams of religion, it fascinates him that he has constantly been close to people associated with institutional religion. His eldest son, Graham, a senior reporter for Reuters in Europe, "was serious and quietly religious from early on. He has now become a devout Catholic. It's very interesting." The authors of two major books on his work, Helen

Dow and Philip Fry, both had strong Christian backgrounds. Explicit religious symbols — crosses, priests, churches — find their way into many of his images. His 1991 painting of a friend, a Baptist chaplain at Acadia University, was on sale for $185,000 in 1995. Although the cassocked chaplain looks severe in the painting, Colville says he's long admired the subject's commitment to students. "I think he has a much greater influence than many people realize, particularly among young people who come here and get into some very difficult situations. He is completely selfless and will spend unlimited time with people. Of course the guy is somewhat of a mystery to me. So the kind of grid that passes between us and him is a kind of metaphor for the inexplicable nature of his function."

He still gives $100 a month to the local United Church, which Rhoda attends regularly. But Colville goes to church only about four times a year. "I recognize that the minister is a good person and he does important pastoral work and he comforts the dying. And I recognize the church is a force of good. I'm amazed at the young couples there with children." While many cherish the community-building efforts of folksy clergy, however, Colville can't stand the moment when the upbeat minister chimes "Good morning everyone" and the congregation responds in kind. When it's time for the congregation to turn to each other in greeting, Colville squirms. "I just *hate* that. I don't want to get involved in that. I find it embarrassing."

As a youth, he was a devout Catholic who attended church daily. But for some reason, his intense religious feelings evaporated when he was eighteen. He casually switched to Protestantism during the Second World War, mainly to avoid offending Rhoda's Protestant mother.

He believes in God, but not necessarily in the divinity of Jesus — a theological stumbling block he shares with many writers and artists. Colville thinks that there has not been a great artist who was also a

Christian since the medieval age. "In my teaching years," he recalls, "I would always get in fine arts some genuinely Christian students. And I would always think they were never very promising. Nice. But not promising. I don't know what the answer is to this now, because obviously in the Middle Ages this did not apply. But I don't think there is any artist of any importance since the Reformation that I would call a real Christian. I feel an artist since the Middle Ages has actually sort of become God. So there can't be any other. You get running it all yourself and there's no room for a backseat driver. A Christian artist has all the answers to the questions and I think that doesn't work for an artist."

I point out that the late primitive Canadian painter William Kurelek was Christian. Kurelek was an exception, says Colville. Kurelek was what he would consider a "real Christian." He was an evangelical Christian with doctrinaire views of an all-powerful God, of an exclusive route to heaven, and of Jesus dying in a singular act of redemption for humanity's sins. "I guess I think of Jesus as a remarkable man. But for me it's like when a person tells you that someone else they know is perfectly wonderful. And then you meet that person and you end up thinking that person is not that remarkable. I feel a little that way about Jesus. I guess I feel he's been overdone. And this has sort of turned me off."

He is friends with many Jews, whom he says are prominent in the art world, and tends to prefer the Old Testament to the New Testament. "I guess I tend to think of Christianity as being sort of soppy and vague. And the Jewish stuff, even the eye for an eye and tooth for a tooth kind of thing, I must confess has a certain appeal for me."

Although Colville admires many Christian clergy and thinkers, such as Hans Kung and Reinhold Niebuhr, a second stumbling block he finds in Christianity is the faith's attitude toward animals, which are central to Colville's life and worldview. Animals, particularly his own dogs, frequently appear in his paintings. Since he believes the nineteenth-century form of Christianity that currently holds sway in the West grants humans dominion over all things, he finds the Jewish approach to animals more appealing. "In the Jewish tradition, the slaughter of animals is a religious thing, done with great gravity, and absolute regret, in a sense."

One of Colville's paintings, nevertheless, shows a positive relationship between a dog and a Christian priest. Sitting together on a dock, staring out at the sea, the dog's head is superimposed over the priest's head. It's a concept Colville picked up from Egyptian mythology, which often depicted humans with animal heads. The painting seems to suggest the dog and priest are one. They are communing with each other, soaking up nature.

"I don't see animals as at all inferior to people. In fact, as I've said, one can't imagine a bad animal." He learned from the Second World War that "the extent of evil humans are capable of is almost beyond conception." He couldn't bear to read about the trial of Paul Bernardo, who was convicted of the torture-filled sex slayings of two Ontario teenage girls. "Nothing like this happens with animals. Animals fight and kill each other, but it's all part of the scheme of things."

Colville believes animals may have souls. "I have no reason to think it's any more likely that a person would have an afterlife than an animal would. And of course there is the possibility one comes back to life in another form."

Suddenly, his own dog breaks the stillness of the summer afternoon by hustling in to the sunroom, panting and sniffing, surveying the tidy scene. Rhoda must have just brought the dog home from their cottage, he says. The maned, yellow crossbreed appears in "Dog and Groom," a self-portrait of Colville on his knees brushing the dog's hair in what seems a reverential way. As Colville pats the dog, he says, "I have actually thought of the possibility of returning as an animal. It would be quite nice."

He imagines heaven as a kind of "frozen state." There is such a thing as too much order, and Colville fears old-fashioned visions of heaven have it. He needs to balance order with liberating creativity. So for him, reincarnation, "being something else somewhere else," is a more alluring possibility than heaven. He barely smiles when he says, "I once said to my wife if I come back I will return as a sort of yellow mongrel dog, medium size."

Carol Shields

"Love is the basic building block. It's your basic molecule."

Wedding energy buzzes in the courtyard of the Pacific Palisades Hotel. "Isn't she beautiful?" Carol Shields asks, after jumping up to hug the slender, yes, beautiful, woman who was about to marry her son. Shields has just flown into Vancouver from Winnipeg for the weekend wedding.

Sitting by Shields on a bench, I was talking to her when her daughter-in-law-to-be walked up. Trying not to invade their private moment of greeting, I turned off the tape recorder and looked away while they hugged.

Later, I wondered whether Shields, the self-confessed "observer," would have looked away. She may well have watched for each human detail: the exact way the hug occurred, the place where hands touched, the expression simmering in the eyes. These ordinary — but exceedingly rich — moments fill Shields's novels, including *The Stone Diaries*, which won both the U.S. Pulitzer Prize and Canada's Governor-General's Award for fiction, and was a finalist for Britain's Booker Prize. When Shields gushed over her son's fiancée, you couldn't have distinguished her from any other somewhat romantic, middle-class mom in a summery beige dress.

Shields wouldn't care. Motherhood and a marriage of more than forty years to husband John, an engineering professor, have shaped who she is. This is a down-to-earth woman from a down-to-earth city who admits she vacuums her house to calm the excitement generated by a halcyon time of literary honors. What sets Shields apart is her talent, seen in books such as *The Republic of Love* and *Swann*, to delve into those ordinary, perhaps sacred, moments with scientific precision, poetic passion, and a priestly sympathy.

The wedding of her lawyer son at Brock House on Jericho Beach includes all the elements Shields values most: meaningful relationships, small ceremonies, and love. Most of all, love — romantic love, self-giving love, and mystical love; love that elevates the ordinary into the extraordinary. Technically, some might call Shields an atheist. But she has intense yearnings about the ultimate things in the universe. She speaks of love, and acts out love, with more compassion and passion than many a clergy member, many a person who speaks easily of God.

"I never used to cry at weddings. But now I do. And the reason is I know what a huge undertaking it is. I didn't used to know," she says in her high, delicate, surprisingly firm voice. All of the Shields's five children, four daughters and a son, were at the nontraditional wedding. The exchange of vows was to occur when the spirit moved the couple, at an undesignated time in the middle of the afternoon party. A judge would preside.

Although Shields taught United Church Sunday school to her children, and took part in Quaker services until 1990, only one of her children, a daughter, has held on to remnants of organized faith. But rituals remain essential to Shields — university convocations, bar mitzvahs, funerals, or weddings. "A wedding announces to the world that there's been a deal struck," she says, laughing. "It's saying there's been a permanent arrangement entered into, and a kind of new adventure. My first book was called *Small Ceremonies*. And even though most of our ceremonies have become secularized, I think ceremony is a kind of spiritual exercise, and spiritual food."

She's initially reluctant to talk about whether everyday life is sacred, saying she doesn't want to sound phony spouting off. Nevertheless, sitting amid the courtyard garden, travelers roaming around with luggage, a big diamond ring on the wedding finger of her small hand, she eventually asks, "What does it mean to be ordinary? I feel we're all ordinary, or none of us is. And I suppose I think none of us is. This is a kind of romantic notion these days. But I think our sense of ourselves, our individuality, is a sort of sacred pattern. Our differences, our uniqueness, our particularity, is a sort of sacred territory."

Shields, who was born in 1935, grew up in Chicago, where she attended Methodist Church. When she married John at age twenty-two, she moved to his homeland of Canada, following him from university to university. (He is now in the engineering department at the University of Manitoba, where she is in the English department.) Like a traditional wife, Shields began to have children at age twenty-three, teaching them Sunday school at United churches in Ottawa and Toronto. She wanted her children exposed to Christianity until age thirteen.

"I have a photograph of myself in the sixties, you know, when everyone was going crazy. And I was standing in the back yard with a hat and a handbag and a Bible. And I was going off to teach Sunday school, which I did for five years. There were a lot of people like me, even though it's not something you think of about the sixties."

However, she eventually grew tired of church sermons, and became a Quaker in the late 1970s. She attended Quaker meetings in Ottawa and for a couple of years in Vancouver. There are no sermons at Quaker gatherings, just silence occasionally broken by short, voluntary comments.

"I found a kind of serenity, I guess. It was sort of a transition, in a way, because a lot of Quakers are Christian. I think everyone should go to a Quaker meeting at least once. We often experience silence. But I had never experienced silence with a group of people. And this was an hour of silence. At first I was looking at my watch and wondering what I would do. So it was kind of uncomfortable at first, but also quite transcendent. I thought it was wonderful."

After moving to Winnipeg in 1980, Shields regularly met with about ten Quakers. But the group dwindled and finally ended in 1990.

"I don't do anything now," she says simply.

Would she like to?

"In a sense. In a sense." Her voice has a touch of regret.

She remembers asking her daughter, who had chosen to be confirmed, whether a crisis of faith caused her to eventually leave the United Church. "She said, 'No. It just kind of evaporated.' And, in a funny way, it did for me too." Shields searches for the best way to describe the transition. "To put it another way, I realized what I'd always known, but couldn't articulate. And that is that God was a metaphor. I suddenly knew that one day. I felt quite comfortable with that."

She's come to nothing, except a kind of humanistic spirituality, she says. She doesn't think about God now. She doesn't think of God as having a body or being an entity. "I don't really. No I don't," she says, continuing to probe her heart to see if she's truly being honest. "I don't think of a mind behind the universe. There is a question mark behind the universe, and I don't suppose we'll ever get to that."

But she has had quite a journey wondering about that cosmic question mark. It was hardly existential *ennui*, or a disturbing death-of-God experience, that she felt during her Quaker silences. "It was the sense that you understand the patterns and how we connect. It was the opposite of feeling alienated. It was the sense that there was an order in the world — sort of a moment when we feel we understand how the world is organized and feel connected to it. I think those are moments of transcendence. This is what poets write about. This is what we're all after. Everyone has these moments of transcendence. But not everybody recognizes them for what they are. And sometimes I think it's because we don't have the vocabulary to describe them. I'm told that English is rather poor in vocabulary for transcendence. I'm told Hindi and Eastern languages have such words."

Shields seems to have more faith in the universe, more trust in the renewing experience she calls transcendence, more trust in the centrality of love, than most. Perhaps someone who has overcome religious illusions is more free to embrace the mystery behind the universe. She now finds her spiritual connection to the universe not through religion, but through literature. "I can't tell you how grateful I am that I am able to respond to works of literature. I've been saved again and again by that blessed — what should I say? — gift."

She is restored, saved from periods of alienation, through language. She loves a story about a New England woman who had an epiphany washing dishes. The woman looked up and on her wrist was a wreath of soapsuds, with a light shining in from the window. And the woman suddenly felt she understood the order of the universe. "It was one of those moments of irrational transcendence. And she called her husband to come into the kitchen to tell him she had experienced this. And he immediately called for the funny wagon to take her away to a psychiatric hospital. It's probably apocryphal, but what it means to me is we don't have ways to express those moments."

She adds, "You must have had those moments."

I guess I have, I say. But I've never articulated them in detail, or written about them.

She watches me, a little concerned. The question seems to hang in the air: Why wouldn't I, a religion writer, write about those transcendent moments?

I should, I say. Her caring, gentle way has turned the tables, drawing confessions out of me. She makes me realize I should be more like an artist, or a mystic, contemplating my experience, mining my transcendent moments for meaning in a more focused way than I do now. It is easier to pick up your ideas from others. Studying your own experience demands more bravery; you never know exactly what you might discover.

For a woman whom it would be perfectly safe to call spiritual, Shields is blunt about what she has rejected of religion. Just as she no longer believes in any orthodox God, she has an atheist's approach to death. She doesn't believe anything happens after death.

"I think it's the end. I'm very comfortable with that. It's certainly nothing I'm afraid of," she says. "Of course, ask me in ten years." She is less comfortable with what comes before death: "The loss of control. The loss of creativity. Pain. Inconvenience to others. Loss of pleasure. Loss of vitality."

She explores this subject and more near the end of *The Stone Diaries,* when she details the final phase of the long, plodding life of her bewildered main character, Daisy Goodwill. Daisy's last unspoken words are "I am not at peace."

From the start, Shields says, the whole of *The Stone Diaries* was written toward that one sentence. "And when I got to that sentence, I had a hard time writing it. I thought maybe I should write, "I am at peace," because my instincts go toward harmony. But I couldn't. I just think too many women, and men too, arrive at old age without having touched their authentic self."

Shields has been repeatedly praised for her insightful writing about women. I tell her she is also sensitive toward male characters, treating them seriously and not as generic jerks. "Oh. Well. Thank you," she says, brightly. "I probably don't think about it as much as I breathe it out from my own experience. Men I know have been generally very good. Which is not to say I don't see vast inequities in the world in gender imbalance."

She offers that her next novel is going to be about goodness. "I've always been interested in saints. I have several books of lives of saints. These are people who have tried to be good for no reason we can imagine. I love these stories. Even though they sound crazy, there have always been people who have tried to understand what virtue means. It's something we don't talk about much any more." There was one unknown saint in medieval France who was simple — clearly what we would call retarded, she says. When he died, they buried him and a golden lily grew from his throat up out of the ground. "It was recognition that he had lived a simple but virtuous life."

Does she think goodness can succeed in the world?

"Yes. I do. I do," she says with emphasis, but in a near-whisper, as if it were not something you're supposed to admit. She believes that mass atrocities are less likely now than in the past, and that most of us are no longer inclined to picnic at public hangings. "I would like to think that despite the terrible setbacks we've had in the twentieth century we are evolving morally," she says. But she is tentative. "This is a very optimistic point of view and I don't always feel this optimistic."

When I tell Shields she comes across in her novels as pro-love, she laughs hard.

"What else is there?" she says. "I think love is the basic building block. It's your basic molecule. Why else would we make an effort to be sort of good in the world and with one another, if it weren't for this kind of mystical connection that holds us together? Why else would we do it?"

She turns to the green plants and black rocks in the garden behind our bench. Love is not only something humans feel, she says. Love is even part of a stone's existence. "It was something I was thinking about when I wrote *The Stone Diaries*. I read an interesting book called *The Blind Watchmaker* by Richard Dawkins. It had this chapter that I loved. It listed the characteristics of organic matter and inorganic matter, of stone. And there was not much difference between them. There are more similarities than there are differences between living and unliving matter."

The reason medieval artists often used lots of flowers and animals to decorate the frames of their paintings of humans, she says, was to amplify their faith in this kind of unity of all things in the world.

So is it love that holds the universe together?

"Yes. Yes. Like a magnetic field."

Is it love that keeps the stone's molecules together, just as it keeps humans together?

"Yes. Yes."